Icons
&
Legends

ICONS & LEGENDS
Copyright © 2023 Dr. Rob Carpenter. All Rights Reserved.

No part of this publication may be reproduced, stored in a retrieval system or transmitted, in any form or by any means—electronic, mechanical, photocopying, recording, or otherwise—without prior written permission from the publisher, except for the inclusion of brief quotations in a review.

DISCLAIMER:

This book is dedicated to helping readers become the best and most iconic and legendary versions of themselves. However, no results can be promised or guaranteed. This book does not contain medical advice. Should you need medical advice or assistance, please seek out a qualified professional.

RMC Lit
New York, New York

ISBN: 978-1-7366155-7-7 (hardback)
ISBN: 978-1-7366155-8-4 (paperback)
ISBN: 978-1-7366155-6-0 (eBook)

For information about this title or for bulk orders, email books@DrRob.TV

Publisher's Cataloging-In-Publication Data

Names: Carpenter, Rob, 1985-author.
Title: Icons & legends: success secrets of the world's most influential celebrities/ Dr. Rob Carpenter
Description: New York, New York: RMC Lit, [2023] | Includes bibliographical references.
Identifiers: ISBN: 978-1-7366155-7-7 (hardback) | ISBN: 978-1-7366155-8-4 (paperback) |
ISBN: 978-1-7366155-6-0 (eBook)
Subjects: Positive psychology. | Self-acceptance. | Self-actualization. | Mind & Body. | Performing arts.

PRAISE FOR
ICONS & LEGENDS

"The wisdom and life lessons you'll learn from this book are profound!"

—**Kayona Ebony Brown**
EMMY AWARD-WINNING SCREENWRITER, PRODUCER, & AUTHOR

"Dr. Rob has captured the magic of media celebrities in a bite-size and inspiring way. The stories and lessons of these stars are words to live by."

—**Bob Boden**
EMMY-NOMINATED TELEVISION PRODUCER, NETWORK & STUDIO EXECUTIVE, COLLEGE PROFESSOR, TEDX SPEAKER, TV HISTORIAN

"A treasure trove of insight."

—**Phil Ramumo**
PRIMETIME TELEVISION DIRECTOR

Dedication

To all of the future icons and legends: give this life the best you got.

Table of Contents

INTRODUCTION 02

PART I
ACTORS **05**

CHAPTER 1
THE ROCK 07

CHAPTER 2
MARILYN MONROE 14

CHAPTER 3
CLINT EASTWOOD 21

CHAPTER 4
LEONARDO DICAPRIO 28

CHAPTER 5
ANGELINA JOLIE 35

CHAPTER 6
MARLON BRANDO 42

CHAPTER 7
GEORGE CLOONEY 50

CHAPTER 8
CARY GRANT 57

CHAPTER 9
JENNIFER LAWRENCE 64

CHAPTER 10

KEANU REEVES 71

CHAPTER 11
SYLVESTER STALLONE 78

CHAPTER 12
LADY GAGA 85

CHAPTER 13
JOHN WAYNE 92

CHAPTER 14
HUGH JACKMAN 99

CHAPTER 15
DENZEL WASHINGTON 105

CHAPTER 16
VIOLA DAVIS 112

CHAPTER 17
HEATH LEDGER 119

CHAPTER 18
HUMPHREY BOGART 126

CHAPTER 19
QUEEN LATIFAH 133

CHAPTER 20
QUEEN LATIFAH 141

CHAPTER 21
SIDNEY POITIER 149

CHAPTER 22
ANTHONY HOPKINS 156

CHAPTER 23
KATHARINE HEPBURN 163

CHAPTER 24
MICHAEL KEATON 170

CHAPTER 25
MICHELLE PFIEFER 177

CHAPTER 26
JAMES DEAN 185

**PART II
COMEDIANS 191**

CHAPTER 27
KEVIN HART 193

CHAPTER 28
CONAN O'BRIEN 200

CHAPTER 29
JON STEWART 207

CHAPTER 30
LUCY BALL 215

CHAPTER 31
CHARLIE CHAPLIN 222

CHAPTER 32
DANNY DEVITO 229

**PART III
DIRECTORS & STUDIO WIZARDS 235**

CHAPTER 33
STEVEN SPIELBERG..237

CHAPTER 34
GEORGE LUCAS...244

CHAPTER 35
SPIKE LEE..251

CHAPTER 36
JAMES CAMERON..258

CHAPTER 37
QUENTIN TARANTINO 265

CHAPTER 38
WALT DISNE..272

CHAPTER 39
STAN LEE...279

PART IV
TALK SHOW HOSTS..285

CHAPTER 40
OPRAH WINFREY...287

CHAPTER 41
BARBARA WALTERS..294

CHAPTER 42
LARRY KING..301

CHAPTER 43
TYRA BANKS...308

CHAPTER 44

STEVE HARVEY 315

CHAPTER 45
JOAN RIVERS 322

CHAPTER 46
WHOOPI GOLDBERG 329

Appendix I: Quotes from Icons and Legends 335

Appendix II: Life Lessons from Icons and Legends 356

WORKS CITED 374

About Dr. Rob 386

INTRODUCTION

I've always been attracted to legendary individuals—to the people bold enough, brave enough, and (sometimes) silly enough to go after their dreams.

I've always been attracted to people who refuse to take no for an answer. To people who refuse to quit. And to people who refuse to believe that "the impossible" applies to them.

In other words, I've always been attracted to people determined to live iconic lives.

But throughout my life, I've never been satisfied with simply gazing at, or celebrating, these iconic individuals. I've never been satisfied with the idea that fate simply chose certain people to be great while everyone else watched them reach their greatness.

Instead, I've always tried to peer behind the mystical curtains that have been built around these people and investigate how they do *what they do*. To see how they bend, break—and yes, even remake—the status quo in their own image.

I've tried to understand these icons' thinking, their emotions, and their life experiences. I've tried to understand their routines, their habits, and their systems. And most importantly, I've tried to understand the wisdom they have acquired for themselves to move mountains and often inspire entire generations of people.

But I've tried to understand this not merely for my own purposes or fulfillment; I've tried to understand this so I could see how their wisdom could be passed on to anyone hungry enough to reach for it—and anyone hungry enough to apply it to their own lives.

This is why I wrote this book—the first in what will be a series of books about iconic figures—so that you can easily and practically learn the life lessons these great icons fought very hard for. And so that you can use the lessons they teach in your daily life to better reach your own personal and professional goals.

Now, I do realize that none of these icons were perfect but despite their flaws, hang-ups, and shortcomings, they still pushed the boundaries beyond what many thought possible, which makes their valuable life insights even more remarkable. That said, I chose not to focus on any of these icons' demons or red flags; instead, I chose to focus on the things that reflect the best of them—*the light in them*—and not the worst.

Because this is a series, each book focuses on icons from a particular field (like entertainment, sports, or music). In this book, I focus on Hollywood entertainers who, more often than not, beat the odds stacked against them to achieve their dreams. Sometimes, these odds meant these icons escaped wretched poverty or childhood abuse, while at other times it meant these icons had to battle constant rejection, abandonment, manipulative people, and crippling self-doubt.

In assembling the icons for this volume, it was difficult to narrow down the list, as there are many inspiring people from whom we can learn, but did not make it in. However, I decided to include each icon in terms of how their wisdom and life experiences spoke to me at the time of this writing. In general, I was moved more by the humanity of these icons—who they were as flesh and blood people like you and me—and not just their accomplishments or the "myths" that were built around them.

Ultimately, you can read this book in just 5 or 10 minutes a day, as the chapters are bite-sized. They each feature a short biography of an icon, their top quotes, their most powerful life lessons, and ways you can apply their life lessons to your life today.

You can also read this book out of chronological order—you can skip around to read about any icon you like—as it is meant to be a lifetime reference manual to help you mentally and emotionally power through to becoming the highest and best version of you. I believe the motivation and inspiration demonstrated by these icons will prove to be quite useful throughout your own journey. So, keeping a copy of this book by your side for easy access will be very beneficial!

It is my sincerest hope that the words and lessons of these icons and legends benefit and bless you—and help you become whatever type of icon or legend destiny has called you to be.

PART I
ACTORS

When we think of icons in the entertainment industry, the first thing that crosses most people's minds are actors and actresses—the legendary television and movie stars who embody action heroes, detectives, medical doctors, and a host of other fun, dramatic, and over-the-top characters.

But what we may not think about when it comes to our favorite Hollywood stars are the life lessons they have learned in getting to the top—and the lessons they've learned as they fought to stay there.

In this section, we will dive into the life stories of the individuals who have graced our screens and made outsized impacts on scores of people and societies. From The Rock to Angelina Jolie, from Clinton Eastwood to Marilyn Monroe—and beyond—we will briefly explore the journeys, setbacks, detours, and triumphs of the entertainment industry's greatest acting icons—and how we can apply the wisdom and life lessons they have accumulated directly to our own lives.

Let's get started.

"One of the most important things you can accomplish is just being yourself."

—The Rock

CHAPTER 1

THE ROCK

Dwayne "The Rock" Johnson is one of the highest paid actors of all time. Not only has he starred in Hollywood hits ranging from *Jumanji* to the *Fast and the Furious*, but his films have grossed over $3.5 billion dollars at the box office and he has amassed over 100,000,000 followers on social media. To say that he has inspired millions of people to live their best lives—and in the process become a legend—would be an understatement.

But before becoming the star he is today—and before he was the champion of World Wrestling Entertainment—nobody could have predicted that The Rock would be the massive success that he is. For example, as a youngster he was evicted from his home, he was cut from his pro football team (leaving him with only $7 to his name), and it was not a foregone conclusion he would "make it" in society.

Nevertheless, The Rock did triumph and, along the way, gained many life insights that we can also apply to our lives so that we can become more successful.

THE ROCK'S TOP LIFE LESSONS

> "All successes begin with self-discipline. It starts with you."

1. Success can only be achieved through systematically disciplining yourself.

    For The Rock, every success he has earned in life is because he has learned to say YES to some things and NO to other things. In other words, his success has been because he has trained himself—disciplined himself, really—into only doing things that will advance his personal and professional goals. Nothing more, nothing less.

    For example, The Rock believes that his grueling workout schedule allows him to develop "a look" that makes him physically attractive for roles, which in turn increases his chances of being cast, making more money, and drawing the admiration of more fans. Without the physique he has built because of his disciplined workouts—which he at times does not want to do—The Rock believes that he would not be a leading man in Hollywood (or a star, period).

What we can take away from this is that self-discipline is crucial to giving us that extra "competitive edge" to be our best so that we can reach our goals. If we simply learn to train ourselves to do the right things even when we don't feel like doing them, we can put ourselves on the path to even greater success.

> "I've always loved the showmanship of professional wrestling. While I love making movies, I love that platform, too."

2. The most successful people always put on the best shows.

Early on, The Rock learned that while "fitting in" makes us feel comfortable, "standing out" is what brings you life's greatest experiences (and rewards). As a consequence, he decided that he was going to put on the best show he could—in meetings behind the scenes, in front of live audiences, or in various movies or business deals. And this meant him adopting a larger than life persona.

For example, The Rock readily admits that his "on stage" personality is his normal personality turned up by 1,000 percent. He believes that if he doesn't tell a story or put on a show or become the most extreme version of himself, few would care who he is.

For you and me, we can learn the cardinal rule of "never being boring" if we want to break out from the pack. Whether you are in an office environment or show business, understanding that the story you tell about yourself is the story others will tell about you—so be sure to tell the most interesting and dramatic version of it (so long as it's truthful).

> "You either play the game or let the game play you."

3. In the game of life, you must understand its invisible rules to win.

One of the biggest open secrets to The Rock's success is that he religiously follows routines—a key strategy that separates the greatest achievers from everybody else. From getting up at 4 in the morning to working out a certain amount of times per week, for example, The Rock knows he can achieve greatness by simply doing the same things over and over again to maximize his productivity and success.

Even if The Rock is filming a movie, for example, he still sticks to his morning routine so as not to give up the secret that fuels the empire he has built. He believes that if he did give up his secret—his routine—his success would be short-lived.

In the context of your life, knowing that there are tried and true formulas (or routines or invisible rules) that you can discover and use again and again will help you get to the next level in your success—and ultimately to the highest levels you are capable of achieving.

> "If something stands between you and your success—move it. Never be denied."

4. In the face of obstacles, focus and tenacity will make you unstoppable.

When you stand in the presence of The Rock, it immediately becomes clear that 1) he lives a "no-distractions allowed" lifestyle and 2) that he will put every ounce of energy into achieving his goals. That is, if somebody tells him he cannot do something—or even if he faces doubts himself—he will move forward regardless of whatever he feels is holding him back.

A perfect example of this is when The Rock first came to Hollywood. People told him that he could only be successful if he "slimmed down." But, true to himself, The Rock rejected this advice and did just the opposite: he bulked up into the walking, talking titan that he is, which helped his career take off (because he literally looks like and plays an action hero).

In your own life, you can do the same—that is, you can become unstoppable if you have the tenacity to be yourself (and consequently reach your goals) even if everyone else wants you to be somebody you were never designed to be.

> "It's you vs. you."

5. Double down on your goals AFTER you have reached your greatness.

While it is easy to think The Rock might coast because he is one of the most famous people in the world and worth hundreds of millions of dollars, the reality is he works even harder at the top of the mountain than he did climbing up it. In fact, it is not uncommon for him to work 16+ hour days so he can continue growing into the best version of himself.

In your own life, even after you have reached your goals The Rock feels you should re-commit and work harder than ever just so you can see what you are truly capable of. And I couldn't agree more.

SUMMARY: LIFE LESSONS FROM THE ROCK

- Systematically discipline yourself to achieve success.
- Always give your best performance to be the most successful.
- Know the invisible runs to win in the game of life.
- Tenacity and focus make you unstoppable in the face of obstacles.
- Continue to double down on your goals even after reaching greatness.

"Anything's possible, almost."

—Marilyn Monroe

CHAPTER 2

MARILYN MONROE

Golden Globe-winner Marilyn Monroe has become one of the greatest icons of all time, still transfixing the world decades after her untimely death. But even though she was an incredible success in Hollywood starring in beloved films like *Gentlemen Prefer Blondes* and *How To Marry A Millionaire*, Marilyn had a difficult life in the short time she walked the earth.

For example, Marilyn lived in an orphanage while growing up, and got married at just 16 years old (to avoid having to return to the orphanage). Shortly thereafter, she divorced her husband before acquiring factory work during World War 2. However, as fate would have it, the factory she happened to join is where she wound up receiving her big break after being unexpectedly "discovered." And the rest, as they say, is history.

MARILYN MONROE'S TOP LIFE LESSONS

> "Success makes so many people hate you. I wish it wasn't that way. It would be wonderful to enjoy success without seeing envy in the eyes of those around you."

1. The downside of achievement is the haters it breeds.

   Marilyn's meteoric rise to the top in the early 1950s earned her not only many admirers but also many haters. For example, some studio heads refused to acknowledge her talent or greatness and therefore decided to underpay her compared to other stars. They also refused to allow her to play roles other than "the dumb blonde," which she became known for after she bleached her hair platinum blonde.

   But in addition to earning Hollywood enemies, she also earned political ones too: the FBI opened a file on her believing that she might be a communist spy under the influence of the Soviet Union (she was not) because of her high-profile associations.

   What we can learn from her experience is that success can be a double-edged sword. On the one hand, it can bring financial and social rewards, but on the other it can make people oppose you out of jealousy, paranoia, or hatred. So, when you get the success you desire, know there are two sides to this shiny coin.

> "Fame doesn't fulfill you. It warms you a bit, but that warmth is temporary."

2. If you only pursue things to be recognized, you will never be satisfied when you get them.

Growing up as an overlooked orphan caused Marilyn to desire more for her life—much more. As a result, her ambition to make it in Hollywood led her to, among other things, not only want to be the biggest actress in Hollywood, but also to participate in risqué publicity stunts to seek more and more attention. Over time, however, she realized that getting the external validation she craved only worked for a little while, then feelings of emptiness kicked back in.

Many people today are realizing the same thing about their desire to be recognized on social media or at work or in other capacities too: they're realizing that the need to be "seen" and "validated" doesn't bring them the security or happiness they thought it would.

The lesson we can learn from Marilyn—and from others who are experiencing the same realizations today—is that we should pursue things for the love of them, not because of the rewards or attention they might bring us.

> "I don't stop when I'm tired. I only stop when I'm done."

3. Fatigue should not be an excuse to give up.

   Marilyn's short life on the earth—she passed away at only 36 years of age—was extremely prolific. For example, she appeared in more than 30 films, owned her own successful production company, and relentlessly trained with theatre coaches throughout her career to improve her acting craft. In other words, lazy was not a word that could be assigned to Marilyn Monroe.

   Yet, like with anyone who is human, she still experienced fatigue, weariness, and the physical, mental, and emotional tolls that come from daily-life and the demanding process of filmmaking. Nevertheless, she continued to pursue her dreams (even if imperfectly) by refusing to give up or give in when she got tired.

   In our own lives, we too will have moments where the pressures to perform (whether at work, school, with family or friends, or in volunteer activities) become overwhelming. But if we put our heads down, engage in appropriate self-care when necessary, and refuse to quit before we succeed, we can accomplish our hearts desires just like Marilyn did.

   > "Keep smiling, because life is a beautiful thing and there's so much to smile about."

4. When you slow the world down, you can see more of the beauty in it.

   Although Marilyn experienced a rocky personal life in many of her relationships—as well as with her battle with substance abuse—

she still found a reason to appreciate the life that she had. After all, she went from being an orphan to an icon in a few short years and left a legacy that people cannot stop talking about today.

Even though some cynics would doubt it today, Marilyn's smile, her emotions, and her love of life were all genuine. So too was her desire to experience the beauty of the world even when the world only seemed ugly.

The lesson for us is that no matter what is happening to us or around us, we can still embrace authenticity and find hope in our circumstances if only we learn to see the good that truly does exist all around us (and even within us).

> "If I'd observed all the rules I'd never have got anywhere."

5. Break out of the prison others have tried to lock you up in.

The expectations Marilyn had placed on her were enormous. Many in the public thought she should just serve as an object of sexual fantasy, for example, while many in Hollywood thought she was only useful if they could earn them an extra buck.

But despite the opinions of the people around her, Marilyn learned to do things her way. She refused to be underpaid. She would not privately accept being known as "the dumb blonde." And she decided to live the life she wanted to live despite people telling her to behave in a certain way.

In your own life, as long as you are acting morally and ethically, you don't have to follow the rules other people tell you to follow. You can dance to the beat of your own drum and not worry if somebody thinks you are crazy for doing it.

SUMMARY: LIFE LESSONS FROM MARILYN MONROE

- Haters come along with the journey of achievement.
- The pursuit of goals loses satisfaction if the focus is just recognition.
- Never use the excuse of fatigue to give up on your dreams.
- The beauty of the world can be appreciated when slowing down.
- Escape the prison others have tried to tap you within.

"I tried being reasonable, I didn't like it."

—Clint Eastwood

CHAPTER 3

CLINT EASTWOOD

C lint Eastwood is a cultural icon whose Dirty Harry films made him an international superstar. He is the winner of numerous Academy Awards and Golden Globes as both an actor and director, and his career in entertainment has spanned a legendary 60 years.

But before being crowned Hollywood royalty, Clint struggled in school with both his academics and behavior before dropping out entirely. As a result, he took odd jobs as a lifeguard, golf caddy, grocery store clerk, and forest firefighter just to make ends meet before he got his big break: an acting contract in Hollywood worth $100 dollars a week that would eventually set him on a path to being a movie star for multiple generations.

CLINT EASTWOOD'S TOP LIFE LESSONS

> "If a person doesn't change, there's something really wrong with him."

1. If you're still the same person you used to be, you have missed out on most of life.

   Clint Eastwood's life and career has been the literal embodiment of change. When he was first introduced to audiences a half century ago, for example, he played masculine action hero roles, but he transitioned over time to directing nuanced films that cut to the heart of what it means to be human (not just what it means to be "macho").

   Throughout Clint's life, he has taken on many new—and different—acting and directing roles, not because he wanted to become legendary, but because he wanted to learn, change, and grow into a better and wiser person. And this is why he never retired from Hollywood—because to him, evolving his skills, emotions, and knowledge as a professional and individual mattered far more than staying comfortable and stuck as the same person year after year.

   For you and me, what we can learn from this is that we should constantly seek to learn something new so that we can be wiser, stronger, and better than we were a year ago or a week ago or a day ago. We should constantly be improving and updating ourselves so that we become nearly unrecognizable to our former selves in terms of the knowledge, skills, and empathy we possess.

> "Fate pulls you in different directions."

2. Life is a puzzle, not a recipe.

Because Clint has allowed his passions to guide him, his life has gone in unexpected directions. Not only did he work odd jobs when he was younger, for example, but even after he got older (and became successful in movies) he became the mayor of Carmel, California, as well as a musical composer.

For Clint, life has never been about following one set path or career formula as society teaches many to do; it has been about finding out what he enjoys most and pursuing these things with every ounce of energy in his body. In other words, his life has been about exploring himself and various parts of the world instead of locking himself into a "pre-set equation" for how he should live or the types of career opportunities he should take on.

The lesson that can be learned from this is that it is completely okay to go off the "beaten path" to live the life that is the most interesting, exciting, and fulfilling to you. Just because many others may opt for the easy or convenient or safe route doesn't mean you have to. Do what you want to in life as fate will never make you live life inside of the lines (if you don't want to).

> "I don't believe in pessimism."

3. Cynics never change the world.

   Clint believes his 60 year plus-career could only have been fueled by optimism and hope, not pessimism or despair. For example, if he was cynical or even a "realist", Clint would have never believed in himself after being rejected from nearly every audition he had for the first 3 years after he arrived in Hollywood.

   For you and me, what we can glean from this that even though it is fashionable to be cynical in today's age (after all, many media and online outlets reward cynics' dark outlooks on life and the world), becoming successful over the long run requires optimism. Only an optimistic person like Clint could have believed he could drop out of high school, be a grocery store clerk, and then become one of the most decorated movie stars in the history of the world.

   While Clint understands that his personal story and success is statistically uncommon, the principle behind it—undeniable optimism and positivity—is truly what makes successful people (of various levels) the legends they become.

> "I'm interested in the fact that the less secure a man is, the more likely he is to have extreme prejudice."

4. Insecure people are often the most judgmental.

   In a world full of so many people judging each other, Clint feels that this is happening because people are insecure about themselves. And he is right. Insecurity breeds not only low self-esteem, but it often causes people to want to negatively lash out at those they misunderstand or who are not like them.

In Clint's mind, recognizing and embracing this life lesson has helped him overcome the haters and critics who have tried to throw various types of shade at him during his career. In our own lives, we can do the same. That is, we can understand that if others attack or troll us, it probably has nothing to do with us, and instead has everything to do with how they're feeling about themselves.

> "If I was not a dreamer, I would have achieved nothing."

5. Only dreamers can change their world—and change the world.

More than any other quality, Clint believes that it is his ability to dream that has created his outsized success and longevity. When Clint dreams, for example, he imagines a movie that could not only be made, but a movie that could change the hearts, minds, and souls of those who watch it. And although this might sound like naive fantasy, his drive to keep dreaming dreams has led him to create films like *Million Dollar Baby* and *Unforgiven* that have shook people to their core.

In our own lives, when we allow ourselves to dream of what could be, we can birth something deeply meaningful into the world. And regardless of whether it is a large or small thing we ignite, it will be important enough to make a difference in our lives—and in others' lives too.

SUMMARY: LIFE LESSONS FROM CLINT EASTWOOD

- Don't miss out on life by remaining the same person.
- See life as a recipe, not a puzzle.
- Change the world by abandoning cynicism.
- Let go of judgment and insecurity.
- Changing the world and your world is the role of dreamers.

"I want you to back yourself into a corner [and] give yourself no **choice** but to succeed."

—Leonardo DiCaprio

CHAPTER 4

LEONARDO DICAPRIO

L eonardo DiCaprio—also known as just Leo—is considered a living legend as his movies have grossed more than $7 billion at the box office and turned him into one of the most sought after movie stars in the world. And his roles in films ranging from *Titanic* to *The Departed*, *The Revenant* to *Once Upon a Time in Hollywood*, have helped define modern cinema.

Leo is an Oscar, Golden Globe, and Bafta winner who has been named one of the 100 Most Influential People in The World by *Time Magazine*. He grew up as the son of an underground comic book writer and dropped out of school even though he was rejected from over 100 roles when he started his career and things did not look promising. However, his early instincts were accurate as he has found incredible success as an actor, producer, and activist for the last 3 decades in Hollywood.

But Leo did not find success chasing or creating trends; he found success being himself and making his own way, which is what he would urge you to do too.

LEONARDO DICAPRIO'S TOP LIFE LESSONS

> "I'm not the kind of person who tries to be cool or trendy, I'm definitely an individual."

1. Real winners stay true to themselves.

   Although Leo has been a part of some of the most iconic movies of all time, he has also turned down roles in other iconic movies too. For example, Leo turned down parts in *The Matrix*, *Star Wars*, and *Spiderman*, among others, because he didn't feel like they were right for him.

   Of course, many people would think that this is crazy—but not Leo. Ultimately, Leo only wants to play parts that he feels he can bring all of himself to, regardless of whether the money is good or if the role is considered "trendy" or "hot."

   The lesson for us is to find out who we are and not let things that seem cool at the moment distract us from living our truth. If we are authentic and true to ourselves in the long run, we will come out on top even if declining certain trendy opportunities along the way doesn't seem to make sense to others.

> "Smile, nod, agree, and do whatever you were going to do anyway."

2. You don't need anyone else's permission to win.

   Leo has been criticized for being an activist for environmental conservation and other environmental causes. And he gets criticized because people tell him he should just stick to acting and not try to shove his views down other people's throats.

   But even though Leo hears these things, he just sticks to his guns—without arguing with anyone—and continues to advocate for his beliefs. For example, Leo doesn't debate or get involved in social media wars over his views, but instead produces cutting edge documentaries like *Before the Flood*, *Ice on Fire*, and *The Right Stuff* to educate others on the impacts of climate change.

   What you and I can take from this is that even if people criticize or oppose us, we can simply smile and continue moving forward with our plans without stopping to brawl with every person who wants to pick a fight. Not only will we preserve our energy and reputation this way, but we will also be much more focused and productive in getting what we need to get done.

> "Pay close attention to the people who don't clap when you win."

3. Always know who is for you.

It might be easy to think that Leo lives in a land of butterflies and bunny rabbits given his success. However, his station in life—rising from being a high school dropout to one of the biggest stars of the millennium—has been hard fought.

But in his rise to the top, Leo has learned that it is not necessarily the people who outright oppose you who are the most dangerous to your mission or success in life. He's learned that sometimes it's the people who are quiet and say nothing at all—especially during your success—who can be the trickiest and most deceitful of all.

The lesson here is that not everybody will celebrate your success—and you will need to understand who they are, why they don't, and how you can limit their access to your life.

> "Only you and you alone can change your situation. Don't blame it on anything or anyone."

4. Once you refuse to be a victim, life becomes limitless.

As mentioned, Leo auditioned for over 100 parts in Hollywood and was rejected from each one of them before he could land an agent. But even after he started getting parts, he still faced rejections from roles. And as strange as it is now to hear, today he still gets rejected from parts.

Nevertheless, Leo doesn't allow this to deter him from moving forward and reaching toward his dreams. Just because he has fame and success doesn't mean he is immune to the psychological or emotional tolls of rejection—or the tolls of public scrutiny and media criticism— but he still presses ahead.

For you and me, when we keep putting one foot in front of the other—on our good and bad days—nobody can stop us from reaching some version of our goals. We will truly become limitless when we don't give our power to other people or allow anything to stand in our way.

> "To join the top 1% you have to do what the 99% won't."

5. Almost everyone knows the formula to success but almost nobody uses it.

Many people think that Hollywood is almost impossible to crack. But not Leo. He understood— even as a teenager—that if he refused to play the odds, then the odds would refuse to play him. In other words, he understood that he had to do things that unsuccessful actors were unwilling to do to put himself ahead of the pack.

Even to this day, Leo is known to put himself in situations that make him stand above his peers. For example, in filming The Revenant, Leo often acted in frozen rivers or slept in animal carcasses just so that he could get "the right shot." Of course, he could have filmed the movie in the studio and used CGI, but what separates Leo from others (filming in nature vs in the studio) is why he is the icon he is today.

The lesson here is that we will consistently have to do things that others are unwilling to do so that we can live the lives of distinction we are capable of.

SUMMARY: LIFE LESSONS FROM LEONARDO DICAPRIO

- Winners stay true to themselves.
- Winning does not require anyone's permission.
- There will always be people for you and against you.
- Life is limitless when we refuse to be a victim.
- Much of success is a formula you can follow.

Nothing would **mean** anything if I didn't live a life of use to others."

—Angelina Jolie

CHAPTER 5

ANGELINA JOLIE

Angelina Jolie is a Golden Globe and Academy Award winning actress who has been declared both the highest paid actress in Hollywood and the most beautiful woman in the world. Her movies range from *Lara Croft: Tomb Raider* to *Girl, Interrupted*, and her humanitarian work has taken her across the globe advocating for refugees and various social causes.

But growing up, Angelina's life was rocky. She became estranged from her family, for example, dropped out of school, became addicted to drugs, and experimented with self-harming and suicide. It wasn't until after being hospitalized for a nervous breakdown in her early 20s that she gradually re-built her life before finding her voice in acting, advancing the rights of others, and becoming a living legend.

ANGELINA JOLIE'S TOP LIFE LESSONS

> "When I get logical...that's when I get in trouble."

1. Sometimes trying to "figure things out" is the worst thing you can do.

   Although Angelina was born to famous parents who were actors, her life did not seem to make much sense early on. For example, she felt alienated from other children around her, which caused her to experiment with drugs and cutting herself, among other things. She did this because she was searching for meaning and identity and, at the time, engaging with these things seemed to make the most logical sense for her.

   However, Angelina abandoned these things because she stopped trying to make sense out of her mess; instead started to make meaning out of it. Put differently, she stopped asking "why" everything was happening to her and instead became intentional about "happening to" things. She began to follow her inner moral compass, for example, which caused her to be a light to the world instead of complain about how much the world hurt her or how unfair it was because it hurt her.

   The lesson we can learn from this is that we don't need to figure everything out to live a successful life (nor do we need to live or perfect life or a "pain-free" life). All we have to do is decide to do what we believe is right—even if it doesn't make logical sense—and let everything else fall into place.

> "I don't see the point of doing an interview unless you're going to share the things you learned and the mistakes you make. So, to admit that I'm extremely human and have done some dark things I don't think makes me unusual or unusually dark. I think it is actually the right thing to do, and I'd like to think it's the right thing to do."

2. Only open your mouth to teach, inspire, or empower.

As a Special Envoy for the United Nations, Angelina has traveled to nations ranging from Kenya to Afghanistan, from Ethiopia to Cambodia, and has seen up close how dark and depraved the world can be. As a result, she understands that when she speaks, she should try to shed light, not heat. In other words, when Angelina communicates she doesn't do it simply for entertainment purposes or to get easy attention; she communicates to show others that life— that the world—can be better if only we will be vulnerable with each other and speak love and truth into humanity.

What we can learn from this is that we should choose our words very carefully. But this doesn't just mean spoken words. It also means written words like e-mails, text messages, and other forms of online and offline communication. When we do we can become vessels of wisdom and warmth like Angelina, which is something the world needs much more of.

> "Anytime I feel lost, I pull out a map and stare. I stare until I have reminded myself that life is a giant adventure, so much to do, to see."

3. The world is much bigger than "your world," so go out and explore it.

Although it can sometimes seem like it is easy to get lost in the big bad world, the flip side of this is that it can also be easy to find something meaningful in this world if we look hard enough. For Angelina, this means not dwelling on the negativity she sees in the news or on social media, but instead overcoming this negativity.

For example, Angelina has searched out the most deserving—and overlooked—areas in the world and has opened up countless schools, medical clinics, and refugee camps in them. She has even opened up schools for girls returning to society from refugee camps who find it difficult to readjust to everyday life.

The lesson for you and me: there is a lot of pain and sadness in the world, but there is also a lot of hope in it if we choose to move beyond what we know and go where we can be of service to others. In other words, if we can expand the world we're "focusing on" to a bigger or different world, we can see how adventurous it can truly be and how much we can help contribute to making it better.

> "We come to love not by finding the perfect person, but learning to see an imperfect person perfectly."

4. True love is not based on perfection, but on perspective.

Over the years, Angelina will be the first to admit that she has had ups and downs in her personal relationships. But with each relationship, she has grown and learned lessons not only for the next romantic relationship, but for all of her relationships.

For example, it was when she was married to fellow actor Brad Pitt that she learned complete self-sacrifice by adopting 3 foreign children and taking them in as her own. She was at the height of her fame and career influence, but decided that loving others was more important than being "important."

For you and me, when we start seeing that true love of others is not expecting or demanding perfection from them, and is instead learning to see them for who they are—warts and all—we will grow into a powerful self-sacrificial type of person that Angelina has evolved into (and add more love into the world that craves it).

> "Jump forward, mean well, commit, and just see what happens."

5. Failure only happens when you refuse to leave your house.

Angelina is the type of flesh and blood icon who doesn't play it safe. From becoming the first modern superheroine by playing Lara Croft, for example, to risking her money to open up refugee camps, Angelina makes bold decisions without getting caught up in "analysis paralysis."

The lesson we can learn is that life can become spectacular when we try to do big things even if it means we might fail at them. For Angelina, she believes we should move ahead with our dreams and let them play themselves out instead of thinking about all the reasons they might not work.

SUMMARY: LIFE LESSONS FROM ANGELINA JOLIE

- Trying too hard to figure things out creates unnecessary problems.
- Put all your efforts to teaching, inspiring, and empowering others.
- Go out and explore just how big the world is.
- Perspective, not perfection, defines life.
- Isolating yourself results in failure.

"What might be a brave choice for you, for another person they may simply not experience fear."

—Marlon Brando

CHAPTER 6

MARLON BRANDO

Marlon Brando is considered by many to be the greatest "Actor of the [20th] Century." His Academy-Award winning career spanned 60 years, for example, and led him to starring in iconic roles in films like *The Godfather, A Streetcar Named Desire, Apocalypse Now, and Superman.*

But before he became a big Hollywood star, he had to overcome a troubled youth. For example, not only was his mom an alcoholic who neglected raising him, but his father was very verbally abusive and told him he "would never amount to anything."

But despite this, Marlon did amount to many things. And he helped others amount to many things too (like when he risked his life, money, and reputation by standing with his friend Dr. Martin Luther King and the civil rights movement when it was not popular—or safe—to do so).

MARLON BRANDO'S TOP LIFE LESSONS

> "If we are not our brother's keeper, at least let us not be his executioner"

1. The lack of empathy is one of the greatest threats to our lives—and to humanity.

As a strong advocate for Dr. Martin Luther King and the civil rights movement, Marlon got to see firsthand the horrors of the plight of black people throughout America. For example, when Dr. King was assassinated and riots broke out, Marlon marched in Harlem even though he knew there were snipers who were looking to kill people that looked like him. But to Marlon, it was more important to show empathy and stand in solidarity with black people than stay home and feel "safe and secure."

Throughout his life, Marlon believed that standing up for the rights of the forgotten should be his number one priority—and he always behaved in that way. Even when he won an Academy Award for his performance in the Godfather, for example, he refused to accept the award because Hollywood was mistreating its Native American workers at the time and he demanded that they be treated more fairly.

The lesson that can be learned from this: we should stand up for the people society often overlooks, even if that means we aren't always comfortable in doing so.

> "We make up any excuse to preserve myths about people we love, but the reverse is also true; if we dislike an individual we adamantly resist changing our opinion, even when somebody offers proof of his decency, because it's vital to have myths about both the gods and devils in our lives."

2. People only believe the story about your life they want to believe.

Because Marlon worked in show business for over half a century, he saw countless people form opinions about him even though they did not know him personally. At the time of his friendship with Martin Luther King Jr., for example, many disliked him because Dr. King was extremely unpopular at the time (even among many black people). As a result of this (and a few other issues), Marlon's popularity declined, as many people did not want to acknowledge all the good he was doing (they only wanted to focus on his unpopular associations).

What you and I can learn from this is that we can't control what other people think about us—or the stories they tell about us. But what we can control is our personal integrity and doing the things we feel in our heart are right to do.

In Marlon's case, he always lived this out. Even though people formed certain stories about him, he still lived life his way and didn't care about changing people's opinions about him that probably couldn't be changed anyway.

> "We only have so many faces in our pockets."

3. You must decide whether you will wear your real face or somebody else's.

Marlon was an American original. Not only did he inspire James Dean and Elvis Presley to emulate him—his bad-boy look, for example, among other things—but he was also unapologetic about embracing who he actually was. In other words, Marlon accepted himself and refused to put on anyone else's mask.

For example, although he had a reputation for being difficult to work with at times, Marlon genuinely wanted to use his fame to bring attention to noteworthy causes. An example of this is when Marlon personally participated in Freedom Rides (which were very dangerous given the hostility toward Freedom Riders, who were sometimes hunted and murdered during their rides) to desegregate the south.

What we can learn from this is that we should get very clear on who we are, what we stand for, and be unafraid of living in our own skin—even if that means putting ourselves (especially our reputations) on the line in the midst of others not understanding or agreeing with the mask we feel most comfortable wearing.

> "Too much success can ruin you as surely as too much failure."

4. Gaining the world can leave you in the same place as losing it.

Because his career was so long, Marlon experienced both huge successes as well as he experienced many difficulties in his private life and relationships given the many temptations his fame presented him with.

Put differently, Marlon discovered the fine line between success and failure, and learned that both leave you in a similar place mentally and emotionally. That is, he discovered that success and failure can reinforce each other by maximizing your vices if you're not careful. This can ultimately cause anxiety, disillusionment, and hopelessness, among other things.

In our own lives, we should recognize that money, success, or the other things society teaches us to chase will not protect us from the downsides of getting too much of these things.

> "I refuse to be a fool dancing on a string held by all those big shots."

5. To achieve greatness, cut the strings of those trying to control you.

Making it in Hollywood—or in any profession—often requires not only many personal sacrifices, but also being controlled or strongly influenced by the opinions of those who are gatekeepers or influencers in said profession. But for Marlon, this was unacceptable.

For example, given Marlon's penchant for spending, he had to take certain acting roles for the money under certain circumstances. Even though critics thought this was beneath him, he refused to listen, as he had bills to pay and would not let their opinions dictate how he should spend his time—or earn his money. Of course, these critics would trash his reputation for making a living on films they didn't think he should be in, but their opinions of him could not dictate what he needed more than their validation: namely money to pay bills.

The lesson we can learn from this is that we should always make the best decisions for ourselves given our particular circumstances. Just because others don't like it or disagree with us doesn't mean they should control what we can and can't do. As long as we are making the best decisions we can make at the time, we should be proud of this and stand by our choices and decisions.

SUMMARY: LIFE LESSONS FROM MARLON BRANDON

- The greatest threat to our lives and humanity is the lack of empathy.
- People believe what they want to believe about you.

- Decide to wear your face and no one else's.
- Gaining, or losing, the world can leave you in the same place.
- You have to relinquish ties to those seeking to control you to achieve greatness.

"Everybody needs a co-pilot."

—George Clooney

CHAPTER 7

GEORGE CLOONEY

George Clooney is a multiple-time Oscar and Golden Globe winner whose acting and directing roles have made him an icon in Hollywood. He has starred in projects ranging from ER to *Michael Clayton, Ocean's 11* to *Three Kings,* and has used his stardom to bring attention and results to important social causes around the world like genocide in Darfur, Sudan.

But despite having massive success, George started off as a women's shoes salesman and construction worker after dropping out of college before landing extra work in Hollywood. However, he parlayed his being on set as an extra strategically to become one of the biggest movie stars in the world after a long climb to the top.

GEORGE CLOONEY'S TOP LIFE LESSONS

> "You have only a short period of time in life to make your mark."

1. Your greatest successes will often come during short seasons of intense productivity.

   Unlike many actors, George rose to fame in his mid-30s—not early 20s. As a result, he had more time to think about how he would—or should—use his notoriety and how long it might last.

   For example, George concluded that most actors have a 10 year window where audiences embrace them before moving on and embracing the next actor. Because of this conclusion, George decided to throw himself into an intense period of work—and humanitarian and political activism—when his star was shining brightest. And when he did this, the results were remarkable: he appeared in dozens of movies, amassed a fortune in the hundreds of millions, and traveled the world to advocate for refugees (all within a period of about a decade).

   The lesson we can learn from this is that we can achieve truly remarkable things if we understand that our greatest successes will often come in short windows of time. Of course, we can achieve success at any time—before or after prolific outbursts of productivity—but if we focus intensely for a season we will realize just how much of our greatness can happen in short order.

> "I had to stop going to auditions thinking, 'Oh, I hope they like me. I had to start thinking I was the answer to their problem."

2. Never think of yourself as a grasshopper, think of yourself as a giant.

It took George nearly 20 years to land a major breakout role on a television show (*ER*). What he learned leading up to that role is this: you have to go into any environment (be it a job interview or anything else) with extreme confidence so that others can be confident in you too.

In other words, George realized that seeing himself as a giant, and not a grasshopper, is what helped him land not only his first major role, but also subsequent roles that turned him into a bona fide legend. It was his confidence—not his competence—that attracted others to him.

Likewise in our own lives, if we start to live confidently (even before we achieve the goals or desires of our hearts) people will take notice and become champions for our dreams.

> "When you're young you believe it when people tell you how good you are. And that's the danger, you inhale. Everyone will tell you you're a genius, which you're not, and if you understand that, you win."

3. Smoke but don't inhale.

George has not only been named the sexiest man alive and one of the most influential people in the world, but he has also amassed a half a billion dollar fortune in the process. And he has won two Academy Awards, 3 Golden Globe Awards, and received an AFI Lifetime Achievement award. Yet despite all of this success, George knows that he is not as good as his resume suggests.

For example, even though people see George as a playboy jetting off to exotic lands, he is the first to admit that he lives a very simple life. That he prefers minivans to Lamborghinis. And that he is not as talented as other people believe he is.

The reason George admits this is not to project false humility, but to be grounded in reality that his professional resume is not who he is as a person. And because he understands this, it allows him to remain open-minded, flexible, and hungry about the future (which are the qualities necessary to win).

What we can learn from this is that we can easily undermine our personal or professional lives if we buy into our own hype too much.

> "It's not about an opening weekend. It's about a career, building a set of films you're proud of. Period."

4. Your life is an entire book, not just a single chapter.

Even iconic actors like George Clooney have had critical and commercial flops. For example, George starred in the film *Batman & Robin* which was, by all measures, not successful. But to him, he did not tie his ego or pride to the failure of this project; instead, he looked at it as a learning opportunity and as a way to always remain humble. He knew that even with the best of intentions, success is not guaranteed.

For you and me, we can also see that if we fail at things—no matter how big or high profile—we do not have to look at that failure as all-defining. We can instead see it as a challenging chapter in a long book that is our lives.

> "Peace, like war, must be waged."

5. Being intentional about every aspect of your life will create positive results.

Although there is a common adage of "go with the flow" as it relates to life, the reality is George believes that going with the flow will leave you in the ditch. For George, be it in acting or humanitarian work across the globe on issues like the Armenian genocide, he feels that being intentional is the number one predictor of if you will be successful or not.

The lesson that can be learned here is that success, peace, happiness, and results all have to be fought for—not passively acquired.

SUMMARY: LIFE LESSONS FROM GEORGE CLOONEY

- Short periods of intense productivity can bring the greatest successes.
- You are a giant, not a grasshopper.
- Decide to smoke, just don't inhale.
- Life is not a single chapter, but many chapters.
- Create positive results in your life by being intensely intentional.

"Destiny is not necessarily something we get out of life, but rather, what we give."

—Cary Grant

CHAPTER 8

CARY GRANT

Cary Grant was considered by many to be the epitome of masculinity, charm, and grace. He acted in over 40 movies with some of the biggest stars in the early Hollywood era, had frequent collaborations with Alfred Hitchcock, and became known as the greatest leading man of all time.

But although Cary was bright growing up, his home life suffered due to an alcoholic father and mother who suffered with mental illness. As a result, Cary devised a plan as a teenager to escape not only from home but also from school so he could pursue his dreams to be in front of the lights.

After convincing his father to let him perform vaudeville instead of attending school, Cary's career started to take off until it eventually landed him in Hollywood. And, over time, he grew into the man everyone wanted to be through parts in films like *I'm No Angel*, *Sylvia Scarlett*, *Bringing Up Baby*, and *Suspicion*.

CARY GRANT'S TOP LIFE LESSONS

> "I pretended to be somebody I wanted to be until I finally became that person. Or he became me."

1. Practice who you want to become.

   Cary Grant—who was born as Archibald Leach in Great Britain—always dreamt of being a movie star. And when he was cast in his first films like *Blonde Venus* and others, he realized that he could be this star - but only by growing into the man he believed he could be.

   For example, he legally changed his name to "Cary Grant" and always maintained a demeanor on and off set that set the tone for him being the personification of grace and a handsome leading man. Cary admitted that even though he didn't always succeed at this, the more he behaved as the man he wanted to be, the more he actually became that man.

   The lesson for us is that whoever we consistently show up as is who we will become. It is a take on "fake it until you make it", but goes deeper than that. It is more along the lines of "believe it until you become it", as when you practice being a certain way, you will eventually embody whoever it is you want to be.

> "No greater honor can come to any man than the respect of his colleagues."

2. Be a pleasant experience for those around you.

Not only did Cary receive an Honorary Academy Award—the highest award bestowed by the Academy of Motion Picture Arts and Sciences—but he also earned the considerable respect of the most iconic movie stars and directors of his generation. Hollywood heavyweights from Mae West to Katharine Hepburn, Alfred Hitchcock to Jimmy Stewart, for example, all admired not only Cary's talent, but his off-screen character.

Cary was known for never wanting to hurt or embarrass anyone, for example, and this greatly impressed and put at ease many people in the entertainment industry who were used to others trying to settle scores with them. But more importantly, it showed that Cary was a genuine person who wanted to sincerely connect with others and do great work.

What we can learn from this: when we exhibit strong character and are easy to approach, easy to talk to, and easy to work with, we will generate great affection from those around us. And when we do, we will have known that we left a personal legacy we can be truly proud of.

> "There's no point in being unhappy about growing older. Just think of the millions who have been denied that privilege."

3. Embrace all of the miles you have traveled.

One of the biggest challenges Cary faced in life—that we may all face one day—is dealing with the loss of those he cared about as he aged. For example, he struggled when a succession of friends passed away year after year as he got older (including Alfred Hitchcock and Grace Kelly).

This experience taught Kelly that you have to enjoy the life you are given—and the people who fill time in that life—as it happens. In other words, Cary learned that he could not become upset with the process of getting older (and all that entailed, including losing loved ones), but could instead more deeply appreciate the life he has lived and the people he has lived it with.

The lesson for us is not to be afraid of aging—even though our culture tries to make us afraid of it by worshipping the youthful. Instead, we should embrace turning 30 or 50, or 70 or 90, and celebrate all of the time (and people) that have made up our lives.

> "It takes 500 small details to add up to one favorable impression."

4. It's the small things that make all of the difference.

The top costume designer in history, Edith Head, once remarked that Cary was the most meticulous and fashionable movie star she had ever worked with. And this was all by design.

Cary believed in being well-groomed because he always wanted to make a great impression—partly because he was from a working class family and didn't have a fancy education—but also because he took the role of being a role model seriously. For example, he would not let himself be photographed while smoking cigarettes (a practice he maintained his entire life until he quit cigarettes all together) because he did not want to promote this negative practice in young people who looked up to him.

What we can take away from this is that it's the small things that we do in life—being considerate of how we appear to others, making sure we don't unintentionally influence them to make bad decisions, etc.—that will end up being bigger than all of the so-called big accomplishments we think will define us.

> "Insanity runs in my family."

5. Your family isn't the only one that is crazy.

As mentioned, Cary's dad was an alcoholic, but his mother was also clinically depressed. As a result, she was committed to an insane asylum, and Cary was told by his dad that his mom had died (even though she hadn't).

But then something happened when Cary was 31: he ended up reconnecting to his biological mother (even though he thought she was dead). And the lesson he learned is that while he initially thought his family was crazy for alcoholism or mental illness, he eventually concluded that they were clinically insane given the severe cover-ups they employed to try to hide things from him.

In our own lives (and families), we can learn the same lesson that Cary did: that our family's might sometimes demonstrate behavior that is not logical or normal, but that we can move forward with our lives and do great things regardless.

SUMMARY: LIFE LESSONS FROM CARY GRANT

- You can become who you practice on becoming.
- Be a pleasant experience to all around you.
- Cherish all the miles you have traveled.
- The little things can be the most game-changing.
- Craziness exists in nearly every family.

"We need to tell each other our stories."

—Jennifer Lawrence

CHAPTER 9
JENNIFER LAWRENCE

Jennifer Lawrence was discovered as a teenager by a Hollywood agent while on vacation in New York City and invited to start auditioning for roles. After convincing her mom to let her move to Los Angeles to do so, she dropped out of school at age 14 and went on to become one of the biggest female movie stars of the early 20th Century.

Jennifer is an Academy Award winning actress who has starred in iconic franchises like *X-Men* and *The Hunger Games*, and has been named the highest paid actress in the world. She is the daughter of a summer camp administrator and has been vocal about supporting healthy body image, especially in young girls, and about being a "regular person" by not buying into having to act like a "celebrity."

> "If something seems difficult or impossible, it interests me."

1. To achieve on the highest levels, you have to think on the highest levels.

   Jennifer left school at age 14—without ever completing her GED—as she was hungry to work on television shows and movies. However, when it was suggested that she "slim down" to make herself more marketable, Jennifer refused. She believed she could be cast in Hollywood without being anorexic or becoming someone she was not. And she was right.

   After quickly getting cast in TBS's *The Bill Engvall Show*, she parlayed that success into being cast into a role that would get her nominated for her first Academy Award at age 19—a nearly impossible feat for anyone, much less a girl originally from Kentucky (as Jennifer was).

   Jennifer then leveraged her success to be cast in the *X-Men* franchise. And she did it all while being told she was too "fat," too "young," and too "untrained" (she didn't take acting lessons then—and still doesn't).

   The lesson here is that anything is possible for us if we think big and go after big goals without compromising who we are at our core. If you do this your success might not necessarily be what Jennifer has achieved, but it will put you in a place where you will be in awe of all that you have accomplished despite the odds stacked against you.

> "It's not until we get older that we realize that other people exist."

2. Wisdom begins when we see the world from somebody else's perspective.

    Self-absorption is common in the entertainment industry, which is what makes Jennifer such a breadth of fresh air. For example, even though she has been named one of the sexist women on the planet by *People Magazine, Maxim, FHM, and Glamour,* Jennifer doesn't buy into her own hype and is instead known for being down-to-earth as she constantly compares herself to doctors and other heroes who do the important work compared to acting (in her words).

    In other words, Jennifer refuses to take herself seriously or even the entertainment industry seriously, particularly in light of there being so many other industries out there solving problems for humanity she feels she could never solve. She feels that seeing the world through a bigger perspective—not one of a world famous movie star—is what allows her to stay connected to the people and things that matter the most.

    What we can learn from this is: no matter how great or successful we become—or think we are—if we see the world from another's perspective, we will see just how much other people are important too. By taking our eyes off of ourselves and our accomplishments, we can attain true wisdom that seems harder to come by these days.

> "Don't worry about unkind people...because you come across people like that throughout your life."

3. Jerks come and go, but we don't have to get bent out of shape by them.

   Jennifer has been a victim of sexual violation, as nude pictures were leaked of her and posted on the internet for millions to see. But even though she was humiliated by this, she realized the people that leaked the photos—as well as viewed them—were simply unkind individuals. She has since refused to let people like them control her emotions (by trying to shame or intimidate her).

   For you and me, the lesson here is that there will always be people who are unkind and who are looking to take advantage of us. They might say or do nasty or unfair things to us, for example, but at the end of the day, we don't have to let what they do control us, or hold us back. In other words, we don't have to get bent out of shape every time a jerk or bully tries to make us uncomfortable, as we will encounter these people at various times in our lives and we don't need to give them any power over us.

> "Things can happen to you but they don't have to happen to your soul."

4. Resilience occurs when you refuse to let pain stay in your soul.

From negative reviews from critics to leaked sexual photos to tripping on the red carpet in front of millions, Jennifer has encountered her fair share of difficult and traumatic moments that could leave the best among us wounded (or at least insecure). But being open to public ridicule has not made Jennifer bitter; it has made her better.

Being a celebrity whose personal and professional life is obsessed over can be exhausting, especially when people see her as an object, not as a person. But Jennifer doesn't let all of the good (and bad) attention negatively affect her, because she realizes the attention is a reflection of the souls of those giving it (and not really a reflection of her).

What we can learn from Jennifer here is that regardless of what others try to put us through, the pain they have inflicted on us is a result of who they are, not who we are. And because of this, we don't have to carry the pain around they've tried to instill in us after they've hurt us; we can get rid of it if we are willing to put in the mental and emotional effort to so that we can be free and healthy.

> "Everything has beauty but not everybody can see it."

5. If we look long enough, we can see how truly special the people and things are around us.

Jennifer has been an outspoken advocate of The Special Olympics, the worldwide movement that organizes sporting events on behalf of people with disabilities. In fact, at age 24, she launched a foundation to financially support this organization as well as other organizations that help overlooked and forgotten people, particularly children.

Over the years Jennifer has helped support The Boys & Girls Club, for example, as well as given millions of dollars to children's hospitals so kids can get the care they need that others will not or cannot provide for them.

The lesson here is that we should support those whose beauty may not be obvious, and who are just as deserving of our love, attention, and affection.

SUMMARY: LIFE LESSONS FROM JENNIFER LAWRENCE

- Think on the highest levels and you will achieve on the highest levels.
- Seeing the world from multiple perspectives is at the heart of wisdom.
- Don't allow jerks to ruin your day or your life.
- Refuse pain; choose resilience.
- The specialness of people and things around us just takes a longer look.

"Sometimes we get so caught up in our day to day lives that we forget to take time out to enjoy the beauty in life."

—Keanu Reeves

CHAPTER 10

KEANU REEVES

Keanu Reeves has been named one of the greatest actors of the 21st Century. Not only has he starred in the iconic *Matrix* franchise, he has also helmed the beloved *John Wick* and *Bill & Ted* franchises too. In his time as a box office star, he has earned hundreds of millions of dollars and the title of "the internet's boyfriend".

After being expelled from high school, Keanu set his sights on being an Olympic hockey player before ultimately turning his interest to acting. He started his career acting in Canada before emigrating to the United States where he found success starring in Coke commercials and various television films like *Babes in Toyland*, *River's Edge*, and *The Night Before*.

But perhaps more intriguing is just how big of a heart Keanu has. Because he lost a child and a spouse to unexpected and horrific tragedies, he knows what it is like to feel pain, and so he has made his life about enjoying his time on earth and helping others. Through his foundation, for example, he has quietly given away hundreds of millions of dollars to better the fortunes of the hurting, particularly hurting children.

KEANU REEVES'S TOP LIFE LESSONS

> "If you can make a woman laugh, you're seeing the most beautiful thing on God's earth."

1. Laughter is medicine every human heart needs.

Keanu has learned that the simple things—not the spectacular things—are what bring deep meaning to life. And he believes that the simplest of the simple things is helping others laugh.

For example, he did a comedic cameo in the hit film *Always Be My Maybe* that is one of the funniest scenes in movie history. In the film, Keanu plays an ultra-charming—and also ultra-crazy—version of himself who woos his new love interest by being incredibly romantic—and violent.

But in addition to making others laugh through movies, Keanu believes it is important that people laugh in everyday life too. As a consequence, he has donated millions to bring joy to suffering children with cancer and has personally volunteered at Camp Rainbow Gold in Idaho to help bring laughter to terminally ill kids.

The lesson we can learn is that no matter how important or successful we are, we should not forget that the simple things like laughter are what really count in life. If we can regularly help others laugh—and laugh ourselves—we can experience one of the biggest blessings we're capable of having as human beings.

> "The simple act of paying attention can take you a long way."

2. The greater your focus the greater your future.

Although Keanu jokes and says that he is just a "dumb guy" (partially because he was expelled from and dropped out of school), the reality is he has learned that the secret to success is not possessing massive amount of knowledge. Instead, he has learned that the secret to success is *applying* small amounts of knowledge.

For example, Keanu is known as Hollywood's "ultimate introvert", and as a result he is always paying attention to others in various ways. Whether it is him watching how his fellow cast members handle a scene or being attuned to specific pain others are experiencing that he can help alleviate, Keanu stays focused on being present so that he—and others—can get more out of life.

What we can take away from this is that even though it can be easy to get lost in our own thoughts, fantasies, or pain, if we simply pay attention to the world around us, we can get more out of it than we realize. By refusing to let ourselves be distracted, we can learn more, get better results, and multiply our contribution to others and society.

> "When you truly understand karma, then you realize you are responsible for everything in your life. It is incredibly empowering to know that your future is in your hands."

3. You are the solution you have been looking for all of your life.

As mentioned, at age 17 Keanu dropped out of high school to follow his dreams. He didn't know where they would take him but he did know it would be further than where he currently was - and further than where he would be if he simply just "hoped" he could one day live his dreams.

By understanding that life is all about what you make of it, Keanu has done things on his terms and has empowered others to do things on their terms too. For example, Keanu loves motorcycles, so he took matters into his own hands to not only buy them, but to help make them according to the desires of his heart. He co-founded Arch Motorcycles to build himself customized Harley Davidson motorcycles—and to help others build customized Harley Davidson's who, like him, were looking to literally ride in their dream vehicle.

For you and me, we can learn that we get out of life what we put into it. If we give it our all, chase our dreams, refuse to quit, and see ourselves as the answers to our own problems we can be more empowered than we ever imagined.

> "If you have been brutally broken but still have the courage to be gentle to other living things, then you're a bad*ss with a heart of an angel."

4. You can still live life as an angel even if you have been to hell and back.

Keanu has seen heartbreak up close and personal. For example, not only did he lose a child to stillbirth, but he lost a spouse to a tragic accident and a best friend (River Phoenix) to a drug overdose. This is on top of his taking care of his little sister who suffered through years of painful cancer.

But even though Keanu has experienced heartbreak, he chose not to let it define him. Instead, he decided to do something about it. For example, he donated 70% of his earnings from *The Matrix*, *The Matrix Reloaded*, and *The Matrix Revolutions* to fighting cancer.

But in addition, he also decided to not become bitter over the pain he has experienced or mistreat others because life has treated him unfairly at times.

In our own lives, we can learn that just because things aren't always fair—or because we might experience pain—does not mean that we have to give in to the darkness of the world and turn on it (or other people) in the process.

> "Sometimes enemies are our best teachers."

5. Our opponents often teach us greater lessons than our friends do.

Although you would think that Keanu wouldn't have an enemy in the world, the fact is because he is a rich and famous celebrity there are always people gunning for him. We won't name names here, but suffice it to say that Keanu has learned much from these people—not only how to avoid or shame them, but also how to beat them and grow from the life lessons they are unexpectedly instilling in him.

The lesson here is that enemies teach us things about ourselves, about others, and about the world that can help us grow into becoming the best version of us if we choose to learn the right lessons from our battles with them.

SUMMARY: LIFE LESSONS FROM KEANU REEVES

- Every human heart needs the medicine of laughter.
- Your future becomes greater with more intense focus.
- The solution to your life is you.
- Being to hell and back doesn't have to stop you from being an angel.
- The greatest lessons often come from our enemies rather than our friends.

"Every champion was once a contender that **refused** to give up."

—Sylvester Stallone

CHAPTER 11
SYLVESTER STALLONE

Sylvester Stallone is a Golden Globe and Academy Award winning actor, writer, and director who is best known for playing "Rocky" in the iconic *Rocky* film franchise. After writing the script for the film in just 20 hours, Sylvester convinced a studio to take a chance on him to play the lead role (as an unknown actor) to much acclaim.

Sylvester then used the success of Rocky to star in other film franchises such as *Rambo*, *The Expendables*, and *Escape Plan*, and in many other crowd-loving films like *Demolition Man*.

Early on, though, Sylvester struggled to get by for many years in his native city of New York. For example, he worked odd jobs at the zoo, as a TV extra, and as a movie theater usher where he was fired for scalping tickets. Nevertheless, he pushed beyond his circumstances to chase his dreams and become an icon.

SYLVESTER STALLONE'S TOP LIFE LESSONS

> "Consider the source. Don't be a fool by listening to a fool."

1. Your success or failure depends on the people you choose to believe.

Even though Sylvester didn't come from a movie star background, early on he believed it was important to only surround himself with the best advice possible as it related to becoming a Hollywood star. So, he decided to immerse himself—but not only in acting.

Sylvester visited the local library in New York to hone his writing skills—which he believed were his meal ticket to success—and he was right. He taught himself screenwriting so that he could write parts for himself and set himself up to be the star of the movies he was writing, which was highly unusual for an actor to do then (and against all conventional wisdom).

For example, he wrote the famous first draft of *Rocky* in 20 hours and quickly had agents offering him hundreds of thousands of dollars for it. But Sylvester would only sell it if he could star in the film, which people told him he was crazy to do—after all, he was a struggling actor scalping movie tickets, so why would he risk turning down a lot of money for a script just to act in it?

The lesson we can learn from this is that when we listen to the right voices—and sometimes the right voice is the one that is only between our ears—we can carve out the unique path to success that may not be right for other people, but that is right for us. Even if people think we're crazy or foolish for following our instincts, they will be the ones who look crazy or foolish when we succeed.

> "I have great expectations for the future because the past was highly overrated."

2. If your past looks brighter than your future, start working toward building yourself a bigger masterpiece.

Although Sylvester was a bona fide star with a personal net worth in the hundreds of millions, he never stopped looking ahead. For example, not only did he create the *Rocky* series, but he also developed the successful *The Expendables* series—30 years later.

Sylvester created the franchise not because he had to, but because he wanted to continue building things which he believed would be great. When most people were retiring (at around age 65), Sylvester was just beginning this series because he wanted to be more excited for his tomorrows than his yesterdays.

What we can learn from this is that even if we have had incredible success in the past, we will never be too old to continue working toward new goals and new dreams. If we always have our eye on the future, the future will always have its eye on us.

> "Once in one's life, for one mortal moment, one must make a grab for immortality; if not, one has not lived."

3. Sometimes you have to put all of your eggs in one basket even if you can't guarantee the outcome.

One thing about icons and legends is that they are exceptionally brave—and strategic. Sylvester embodies this in that he has time and again put his money, reputation, or career on the line to invest in projects—and people—he did not know would be a success.

For example, Sylvester revived the Rocky franchise in the 2010s with a new rendition called Creed. But he decided he would not be the leading actor—and that he would not direct the film either. Instead, he cast a relatively unknown actor—Michael B. Jordan—and hired a very unknown director—Ryan Coogler—to make the film. And his instincts paid off. Big time.

Creed became an incredible box office success and also helped launch the actor and director to greater heights (i.e., setting them up to act and direct one of the biggest blockbusters of all time, *Black Panther*).

For you and me, we will sometimes have to use our instincts and place our bets on projects or people that are not a guaranteed success, but who we nevertheless believe could be spectacular. If we are willing to take a chance on them, they just might surprise us.

> "I stopped thinking the way other people think a long time ago. You gotta think like you think."

4. Success comes from breaking away from the crowd, not following it.

Sylvester is not only the only actor to have starred in the number one box office hit across 5 decades (for each decade), but he is also one of the only actors to create multiple franchises worth nearly a billion dollars—or more than a billion dollars per franchise. And he did this because he didn't think like most people—and because he didn't think like most other actors either.

Sylvester had a vision and wanted to be in control of that vision even though nobody before him had ever done what he did. After all, there are many movie franchises today, but almost none of them were created by the actor that bears their name.

What we can take away from this is that breaking from the crowd sometimes means that there might not have been somebody who has ever done what we've done before—and that's okay. As long as we stay true to the vision inside of us we can become who we were created to be, not just a carbon copy of somebody else.

> "I believe any success in life is made by going into an area with blind and furious optimism."

5. Energy and optimism are two of the most overlooked aspects of success.

Nobody would have thought that a former zoo employee and movie usher who was fired for scalping tickets would become a legend in the entertainment industry. But this is what happened for Sylvester. It didn't happen because he was the best looking or most talented or smartest person. It happened because he got excited over his ideas and career and dreams and followed them even in spite of many obstacles.

For example, on his rise to the top things got so bad for Sylvester that he had to sell his beloved dog outside of a liquor store just so that he could buy food to survive for the week. But Sylvester was able to buy this same dog back after he sold Rocky—for $15,000 dollars—and much begging.

The lesson here is that even though our dreams may seem like nightmares at times, if we continue forging ahead with furious optimism we can get some version of the happy ending we've been searching for.

SUMMARY: LIFE LESSONS FROM SYLVESTER STALLONE

- Who you choose to believe will determine your success or failure.
- Always believe that your future will be brighter than your past.
- Even if you are uncertain about the outcome, put all of your eggs in one basket anyway.
- Break away from the crowd for true success.
- The two most underappreciated facets of success: energy and optimism.

"You have to be the antithesis of the status quo. You have to work against it."

—Lady Gaga

CHAPTER 12

LADY GAGA

Lady Gaga is a multi-time Grammy, Oscar and Golden Globe winner, Guinness World Records Holder, and musical phenomenon who has sold more than 100 million albums netting over $500 million in sales. She has been named Woman of the Year by *Billboard Magazine* and is known for her over-the-top image and promotion of being 100% authentic.

Early on, music always came easily for her. For example, starting at the age of 4, Lady Gaga— born Stefani Germanotta—started playing the piano, which eventually set her on the fast track. Fast forward and she was enrolling in NYU's Tisch School of the Arts before she was legally eligible to and then releasing the world's #1 best-selling single before the age of 23.

But true to her values, Lady Gaga believes the most important thing she can do is give back to humanity so she has set up the Born This Way Foundation to advance the rights of the overlooked and underserved. Her empathy to help others partly stems out of her experience of being raped at age 19. Hence, she understands the pain of her fans—who she calls "Little Monsters"—and all they have had to overcome. She wants to help empower them in whatever way she can.

LADY GAGA'S TOP LIFE LESSONS

> "If you don't have any shadows, you're not in the light."

1. Recognizing there are things you must change about yourself is the first step to living peacefully with others.

    If Lady Gaga wasn't a pop star, she would probably be a philosopher given the amount of time she spends thinking about the yin and yang of people. That is, given the amount of time she spends thinking about both the good and the bad people possess.

    For example, many of her songs, ranging from "Poker Face" to "Bad Romance" and beyond, feature the deep contradictions people face within themselves. In other words, many of her songs emphasize that it is possible for people to be both darkness and light at the same time, and that until you recognize this reality, you won't ever try to move toward the light (because you will be stuck in the darkness).

The lesson that can be learned from this is that everyone carries traits that are helpful and hurtful—to themselves and others—and it is only when we acknowledge that we carry hurtful traits that we can begin to live with respect and humility toward others and ourselves.

> "I want people to walk around delusional about how great they can be—and then fight so hard for it every day that the lie becomes the truth."

2. The positive thoughts you think about yourself can override your negative or average circumstances if only you'll apply what you believe.

Similar to other young artists, Lady Gaga truly believed from a young age that she would be a superstar. And then she acted on making that belief a reality.

For example, she dropped out of NYU's Tisch School of the Arts in her second year to pursue her dream of singing full time. This may not have made sense to her classmates—after all, the Tisch School is considered one of the best schools in the world for the arts—but Gaga believed so strongly in her ability to make it that even the world's top arts institution could not contain (or mold) her ambition or talent.

What we can learn from this is that the adage of mind over matter is more common in icons than it is in the everyday public. Few would have the audacity to believe they could live their dreams, but the few that do—like Gaga—often make their dreams a reality. If we start to think bolder thoughts about ourselves, our careers, and our dreams, we can achieve things others will think we are delusional for even thinking about (if only we will think these thoughts while we hustle to make them a reality).

> "Brushes with darkness won't help you create your destiny."

3. Playing with fire burns the bridges you need for your future.

Although Lady Gaga fully embraces the pain of her past—and the pain of others—she does not believe that that pain should stop you from fulfilling your destiny. Nor does she believe that you should medicate that pain by running to easy escapes.

For example, Gaga admits that she has experimented with drugs like heroin and cocaine, but is not proud of it. And in fact, she actively discourages her fans—especially her younger fans—from doing it as she said it only leads to destruction.

For you and me, what we can realize is that just because we can do something dark—or just because we have access to do something dark—doesn't mean that we have to. No matter how easy it is or glamorous it is marketed as, the reality is we should avoid dark things whenever possible as the consequences can be more dangerous than we realize.

> **"Celebrate the things you don't like about yourself."**

4. Using reverse psychology will help you see that your perceived flaws aren't really flaws at all.

In school, Lady Gaga was called a "weirdo" and a "freak" and made to feel like she didn't belong. As a result, she ran to her music to help her heal and process her feelings about it. And what she concluded as she did was that the same things people made fun of her for would eventually lead her to global stardom.

For example, Lady Gaga's theatrical costumes, award show entrances, on stage performances, and public persona are considered unusual, avant garde, and so outlandish that people can't help but be mesmerized by them. Even when she met President Barack Obama for the first time, she wowed him as she wore 16 inch hills, making her stand head and shoulders above everybody else in the room (literally and figuratively), including the President.

What we can learn from this is that the same things that we think are our weaknesses—or that we are embarrassed about—may turn out to be our greatest strengths if only we will look at them in the right way and turn them into our strengths.

> "I don't want to be a celebrity, I want to make a difference."

5. Only you can decide if your life will be about success or significance.

Lady Gaga, whose net worth is nearly $300 million, believes that the most important contribution she can make to the world is not her fame but instead her philanthropy. And by philanthropy, she doesn't just want to impact the world with her money—she wants to impact it with her ideas and emphasis on love and tolerance for people who are different from the norm.

The lesson here is that even attaining the most success in the world will not fulfill us the way giving back will. So, we should set our sights not on making the most money or getting the most likes, but instead on helping as many people as we can as a life and career goal.

SUMMARY: LIFE LESSONS FROM LADY GAGA

- Living peacefully with others requires seeing things you need to change about yourself.
- Positivity of mind overrides negativity and helps change your circumstances.
- Be careful about accidentally burning bridges for your future.
- Your perceived flaws may not be flaws at all.
- Decide that your life will be about success and significance.

"You're short on ears and long on mouth."

—John Wayne

CHAPTER 13

JOHN WAYNE

Marion Robert Morris—better known by his stage name, John Wayne—was an Academy Award-winning actor and Academy nominated director. For nearly 3 decades, he graced the silver screen as one of America's most beloved entertainers, starring in nearly 200 film roles.

Perhaps more than anything else, John became known for his unabashed patriotism and belief in American exceptionalism. During World War 2, for example, he attempted to personally enlist to fight against Adolf Hitler and, decades later, made an anti-communist film supporting the unpopular Vietnam War.

Although John expressed a few beliefs he shouldn't have (i.e., narrow minded views about blacks in line with the views of his generation), he nevertheless added more positive than negative to the world. As a result, the lessons he learned in his life made him one of the greatest icons and legends in history.

JOHN WAYNE'S TOP 5 LIFE LESSONS

> "Courage is being afraid and going on the journey anyhow."

1. Even if the odds don't look good, roll the dice anyway.

John believed in using his career and fame to express wholesome values on screen even though it was becoming increasingly unpopular to do this in Hollywood. For example, John refused to play roles that he felt were degenerate and could negatively impact children's or society's beliefs of behaviors. That said, he was still called out for it even though he was the biggest actor in the world.

For example, some of the most successful stars in Tinseltown criticized John, both in the media and to his face, for not exploring the uglier side of life in his roles. But true to himself, John did not allow his critics' pressure to deter him from trying to be a positive role model for Americans in how he portrayed his movie characters.

What you and I can learn from this is that even if some other people—and society around us—is de-evolving to a darker place, we don't have to devolve with it. Yes, we might face criticism, but we have to have the courage to bet on our beliefs—and to allow those beliefs to go on a journey that at times will encounter enemy fire.

> "When you stop fighting, that's death."

2. Quitting isn't failure, it's surrender.

During World War 2, Hollywood sent more movie stars and directors to war than any other generation in its history. John personally got caught up in this, and wanted to enlist as an infantryman so we could fight on behalf of his country—and take down Adolf Hitler.

However, given his growing popularity—as well as movie studio contracts—Hollywood executives were not pleased that he wanted to risk his life to go overseas and help win the war. As a consequence, they threatened to sue John if he did enlist. Nevertheless, John found a way to fight in a different way.

Instead of fighting for his country on the battlefield, for example, he decided to support the troops by deploying for months at a time to uplift service members on military bases. Although this is more common in today's world, it was not during World War 2. John felt that if he quit on trying to help his county during war time he would be surrendering his integrity and that was too heavy of a cross for him to carry.

The lesson from this is that even if one door closes we want to walk through, we can go through another door and fight for what we believe in even if it is a completely different way than we originally imagined.

> "I'm responsible only for what I say, not for what you understand."

3. You never have to explain yourself to those unwilling to "hear" you.

As mentioned, John was not shy about expressing his beliefs or patriotism for America. While this did not earn him friends who did not want to understand his reasoning, it did earn him unexpected admirers.

For example, although both the governments of the Soviet Union and Imperial Japan were the sworn enemies of the United States, its leaders were personal fans of America-loving John Wayne. So, when the heads of states from these countries came to the U.S., they personally requested to meet with John Wayne, as they wanted to seek out his views on various issues.

What can be gathered from this is that while some may not want to understand your beliefs, others will. We should never waste our time on those who simply want to ignore what we have to say or cancel us.

> "I have tried to live life so that my family would love me and my friends respect me."

4. Being a hero to those who know you best is the sign of a life well lived.

Like many other Hollywood stars, John sometimes had a stormy love life. For example, one of his wives got so angry at him after he came home from a movie party that she attempted to shoot him as he walked in the front door—and thankfully she missed.

Nevertheless, John was respected and loved by his children who expressed their ultimate admiration for him: they followed him into the entertainment industry by attempting to emulate the kind of man—and professional—he was. For example, his youngest son Ethan and granddaughter Jennifer acted and performed in a country music group, respectively.

The lesson here is that the ultimate sign of love and respect is when those closest to you want to be just like you. And in this regard, John was the ultimate hero.

> "Tomorrow hopes we have learned something from yesterday."

5. Your future doesn't need to be a blank canvass.

Although John never finished studying at the University of Southern California due to an accident, he nevertheless was a very intelligent person who loved to learn. And he especially loved to learn about history and from his mistakes.

One of the reasons why he appeared in so many cowboy movies, for example, was not because America was a frontier nation in the 1940s and 1950s; it was because America was a frontier nation in the 1840s and 1850s. In other words, America was historically something that fascinated John to learn more about and portray. He wanted to take the lessons of history and present them to his generation so that they never forgot them.

In our own lives, if we learn from not only our own personal history—but from the history of society around us—we can live more interesting lives just like John. Whether we are more knowledgeable, better conversationalists, or better leaders or artists, learning the right lessons from yesterday will always produce a better tomorrow.

SUMMARY: LIFE LESSONS FROM JOHN WAYNE

- Roll the dice regardless of whether the odds look good or not.
- Don't surrender by quitting.
- There is no need to explain yourself to people who refuse to listen.
- Be a hero to those who know and love you best.
- A blank canvas doesn't have to define your future.

"Respect motivates me, not success."

—Hugh Jackman

CHAPTER 14

HUGH JACKMAN

Hugh Jackman is an Emmy Award winning movie star best known for playing Wolverine in the hit *X-Men* film franchise. But in addition to performing on the big screen, Hugh has made a successful name for himself on Broadway, starring in musicals ranging from Beauty and the Beast to Oklahoma! and beyond.

However, it was not a foregone conclusion he would make it in entertainment much less become an icon. In his early acting classes, for example, he felt he was far inferior in talent to his peers, and growing up in Australia was not exactly the easiest place to get discovered, especially as the son of an evangelical accountant.

Nevertheless, Hugh found his way to Hollywood after a successful audition for *X-Men* and the rest has been history. Starring in films ranging from *The Prestige, Eddie the Eagle,* and *The Greatest Showman* have given him the platform to live the life of his dreams.

HUGH JACKMAN'S TOP 4 LIFE LESSONS

> "If you back down from the fear, the ghost of that fear never goes away."

1. Quitting defeats more people than losing does.

It is easy to believe that an icon like Hugh has never been afraid of anything. But that isn't true. Hugh has faced many fears, including moving halfway across the world to pursue his dreams; re-creating himself for movie roles like Wolverine that fans demanded perfection from; and deciding to sing and dance on Broadway even though he is one of the biggest action stars in the world.

In facing his own decisions to do these things, Hugh was not guaranteed success— or self-confidence. However, every time he faced them head on, he chose not to back down because of fear or naysayers or doubt; he went after what he wanted, believing that quitting on his dreams (as crazy or illogical they might be to some) would hurt him more than pursing them.

The lesson here is that if we quit going after the desires of our heart, we will defeat ourselves. And the most ironic part about this defeat is, the desire will not fully go away; it will remain, but shrouded in pain and regret. This is why Hugh believes that we must run toward our fears, not away from them.

> "Anyone who thinks they're indispensable is fooling themselves."

2. There is only one master of the universe and it is not you or me.

Despite being named "The Sexist Man Alive" by People Magazine and holding a Guinness World Record for playing the longest-running action hero, Hugh does not believe he is indispensable. In fact, he believes that body is.

Hugh's career in entertainment has convinced him that the people who think the world can't run without them are usually the ones it can most run without. For example, some of the people Hugh worked with early in his career seemed invincible only to realize that, once their true characters were exposed to the world, it would take less than a few days or a few hours before nobody in Hollywood would ever want to work with them again.

What we can learn from this is that regardless of how skilled we are, how much money we make, or how important we think we are, professionally we can be replaced in a heartbeat. While this thought might seem scary to some, it should keep us humble, hungry, and ready to do whatever it takes to improve ourselves because somebody will always be waiting to eat our lunch if we are not careful.

> "I'd sell my soul for a good cause."

3. One of the greatest rewards in life is investing all of yourself to improve other people's lives.

Hugh believes in using the blessings he has been bestowed to help others improve their lives. For example, he has used his social media to ask fans to recommend charities he should donate considerable amounts of money to. In the past, he has given to Charity Water and other great organizations using this technique.

But in addition to personally donating, he has also quietly raised millions of dollars for causes like Broadway Cares. He has also started multiple businesses whose sole purpose is to uplift millions of people around the world by selling coffee online through multiple cafes.

Even though this might seem "normal," Hugh is doing this not because he has to, but because he wants to. It is not about getting "credit" or publicity; it is about loving others enough to use whatever resources he has to support them.

The takeaway here is that, whether we have lots of resources or few of them, we should quietly attempt to do whatever we can to lift up those whose lives are more difficult than our own.

> "Your religion should be in your actions."

4. Thinking we are "good people" is not enough; we actually must become the best version of ourselves.

Although Hugh is a Christian and has daily practiced Transcendental Meditation for decades, he believes that actions are more important than beliefs. In other words, he believes that if your beliefs do not make you a kinder and better person toward others, they are useless.

For example, behind the scenes Hugh Jackman has acquired the nickname "Nicest Guy in Hollywood" and he has been faithfully married to his wife - whom he personally made her wedding band for—for 30 years. And none of this is by accident; Hugh works hard to value others and in turn they value him.

The takeaway is that we should let our spiritual, philosophical, and other beliefs transform us so that we personally live them on a consistent basis. Now this does not mean we won't make mistakes or slip up from time to time, but it does mean that most of the time our good actions reflect our good beliefs.

SUMMARY: LIFE LESSONS FROM HUGH JACKMAN

- People are defeated more by quitting than by losing.
- The master of the universe is neither you or me.
- Invest in your life for others and you will reap the greatest rewards.
- Become the best version of yourself; don't settle for "good enough."

"You have to grab moments when they happen."

—Denzel Washington

CHAPTER 15

DENZEL WASHINGTON

Denzel Washington is a former sanitation worker and post office clerk who rose to international superstardom in Hollywood and on Broadway. Although he was a lackluster student and decent college basketball player, he didn't discover his true passion until he took a job at a YMCA summer camp and was encouraged to try acting out.

After graduating from college, he spent several years working on stage as a performer before he got his big break playing Dr. Phillip Chandler in NBC's *St. Elsewhere* for 6 seasons. And, after this, the rest was history: Denzel won his first Academy Award in 1989 for his role in the movie *Glory*, and many other awards for roles in movies ranging from *Training Day* to *Remember the Titans*.

> "You pray for rain, you gotta deal with the mud too. That's part of it."

1. Every dream you have will at times require you to walk through a nightmare.

Despite his Oscars, Tonys, and Golden Globes, Denzel remembers what it was like to live life outside of the limelight. For example, in addition to being a sanitation worker and postal clerk, he was also a garbage man and worked manual labor in a factory. And he did these things to support himself financially so that one day he could live his dreams.

But in addition to the sacrifice Denzel made preparing himself for his dreams, he also had to sacrifice once he reached his dreams. For example, he has had to put up with big Hollywood egos; paparazzi and stalkers; rumors and innuendo; and so many other things that were at best annoying and at worst life-threatening. But Denzel believes that these things come with the territory of being an icon and so it is a necessary and unfortunate part of his job.

For you and me, we will have to recognize that every dream also includes a potential nightmare. But we shouldn't let any potential downsides of a dream deter us from reaching for the upsides of it.

> "The chances you take, the people you meet, the people you love, the faith you have. That's what's going to define you."

2. The people who get the most out of life are the ones who embrace all of its unexpected surprises.

Denzel Washington is a devout Christian, reads the Bible daily, and has often thought about becoming a pastor and a preacher. As a consequence, he doesn't believe anything that happens in life is a coincidence or happens by chance. He believes that there is a greater purpose behind what we call life and that we are given a set of choices that will help us or hurt us - even if we never planned on being in certain circumstances that will require us to make a life-defining choice.

But in Denzel's own life, he is constantly looking for the meaning behind the decisions he has to make in surprising situations he sometimes finds himself in; why people enter and exit his life; and how even his difficult choices can help make him a better and stronger person - not just a more successful person.

The takeaway for us is that no matter how great or rich or successful we become, the truth is what will really define us are the (sometimes surprising) decisions we have to make over time to be the best version, or the worst version, of ourselves.

> "To me, success is inner peace."

3. A heart full of joy is better than a bank account full of money.

Denzel knows the world measures success on how shiny somebody's name is or how fat they can make their bank account.

And he knows that although he has both a shiny name and fat bank account, they are not what make him a true success.

For Denzel, what makes him a true success is knowing that he is a good husband and father. What makes him a success is knowing that he treats everybody with honor and respect. And what makes him a success is having a peace inside of himself despite the ups or downs of his life (and he does have ups and downs despite his fame and fortune).

What we can learn from this is that regardless of what society thinks is "success," true success is simply doing the simple things in life right (the things you probably won't get an award for). In other words, when we strive to be respectful to others (including others who are different from us), we will walk around with a sincere joy and quiet confidence that outward success can never give us.

> "Man gives you the award but God gives you the reward."

4. The blessings you receive now are nothing compared to the blessings that are to come.

Because Denzel's father was an ordained preacher, he was taught to take the long view of life - the one that looks beyond the here and now to something far greater. And as a consequence, this helps him not to dwell on the things that seem to matter in the immediate moment, but instead on the truly important things that will matter down the road.

For example, Denzel has often said his greatest project in life is not a new movie, but instead raising a family that is mentally and emotionally healthy, and that knows they are loved despite their failures or successes. And this is his greatest project because he knows that, in the long run, the most important gift he can give to the people he cares about the most is psychological stability and unconditional love (a gift far superior than an inheritance of flashy homes, cars, or toys).

In our own lives, when we take the long view on life, we will start to see that much of what drives us in our present moment will lose its value if we put things in the proper context. And this perspective should give us peace.

> "My ultimate life dream project is my kids. My family."

5. We reproduce what we are, not who we think we are.

As mentioned, Denzel really loves his children and his family. And it shows.

For example, all 4 of Denzel's kids have followed him into the entertainment industry, not because they wanted riches or fame like their father, but because they admired the good man the industry ironically helped him become. And they wanted this for their own lives.

For you and me, when those who know us best want to be like us there is no higher compliment in the world. After all, we can only reproduce who we actually are, not who we want people to think we are.

SUMMARY: LIFE LESSONS FROM DENZEL WASHINGTON

- Sometimes to achieve a dream you must experience a nightmare.
- Covet the unexpected in life.
- You must choose joy over money to live a meaningful life.
- The blessings of the future will dwarf the blessings of the past.
- WHAT we are, NOT who we THINK we are, will be reproduced.

"When you see what the deficit is, then you have to do **something** about it."

—Viola Davis

CHAPTER 16

VIOLA DAVIS

Viola Davis is the first African American woman to achieve the triple crown of acting, having earned an Academy Award, Tony Award, and Primetime Emmy Award. She starred in the hit ABC show *How To Get Away With Murder*, the movie *The Help*, Marvel's *Suicide Squad*, and many other notable films. As a result of her success, she has been named by *The New York Times* as one of the greatest actors of the 21st Century and by *Time Magazine* as one of the most powerful people in the world.

But growing up, Viola's life was anything but fabulous. She was born on a plantation as the daughter of a maid and when her family moved, she had to share a rat-infested apartment in an environment of pure dysfunction.

But Viola also had to battle with her weight, body image issues, and with stereotypes about black women not "being as beautiful" as others growing up. Nevertheless, she followed her dream of acting on Broadway and Tinseltown, and has become one of the most iconic actors of all time despite people telling her she wasn't "pretty enough."

VIOLA DAVIS'S TOP LIFE LESSONS

> "When you pray, God puts people in your life to lead you where you cannot lead yourself."

1. Your journey to greatness is meant to be taken with others.

   Because Viola grew up in abject poverty, being an actress—or artist of any kind—did not seem like a viable career choice. After all, her home was filled with much dysfunction and was in survival mode for most of her upbringing.

   However, when Viola enrolled in the Young People's School for the Performing Arts, her talent for drama was immediately recognized by its director, Bernard Masterson. Without his recognition and support, Viola does not believe she would have been encouraged to develop and pursue her creative passions to become the star that she is today.

   The lesson that can be learned here is that sometimes it takes the nudge of other people to help you become who you are meant to be. If you ask God to grant you your dream, He will likely send a person—or people—who will help you reach that dream (even if you don't initially recognize them as being the ones He sends).

> "Even when I get the fried chicken special, I have to dig into it like it's filet mignon."

2. Treat everything you do with class.

Hollywood casts roles based on stereotypes and looks. And for Viola, she experienced the downsides of this in terms of the roles it has tried to cast black women in.

For example, Viola found herself being cast in roles playing uneducated black people more often than she can count. Nevertheless, she treated each role with dignity, respect, and honor, and allowed her acting to speak for itself.

An example of this is when she starred in the movie *The Help* playing the role of Aibileen Clark, a maid in 1963 Mississippi, who served an a white family. Even though Viola felt she was in a demeaning position playing a maid, she gave her all to the role and was even nominated for an Academy Award for Best Actress in it.

What we can take away from this is that we can turn even the smallest and most despised things into spectacular masterpieces if we apply our talent and focus to them. Instead of only showing up half-heartedly for things we feel are beneath us, if we always give our best, we can create something special.

> **"The privilege of a lifetime is being who you are."**

3. The greatest reward you can ever receive is recognizing how special you truly are.

As an actress, Viola is always having to play "somebody else." But outside of acting, she doesn't believe that she has to transform into playing the role of "movie star"—or into any other person people tell her she should be.

For example, Viola still loves to shop at Walmart, she still loves to attend church, and she still loves to be outspoken about not having to be a certain body weight—or shape—to feel like an attractive woman in society (or on film). In other words, Viola has embraced who she truly is—a regular person with extraordinary gifts—who is just trying to live her best life without conforming to other people's expectations.

In our own lives, we can follow this model by not trying to pretend to be who we are not. We don't have to keep up with the Jones or Kardashians, we don't have to give up the things that make us happy, and we don't have to hide our true selves from the world. If we follow Viola's advice, we will realize that we truly are *good enough*.

> "Artists can only be truth tellers."

4. The world needs you to tell the truth about it.

   Viola loves embodying characters that tell the depth, sophistication, and complex humanity of black women—and of people in general. In films like *Windows*, for example, and *Ma Rainey's Black Bottom*, she personifies truth and beauty in extraordinarily thrilling ways (matching truth with drama and popcorn thrills). And she does so not simply because she wants to: she does this because she feels compelled to reveal to society real life people and situations that you and I can relate to so that we can be simultaneously entertained and empowered.

   What we can learn from this is that it is okay to speak our minds so that we embody and advance the truth others need to see so that they can grow in their lives. And not only will this be liberating for us, but it will help bring hope to people in society who desperately need it.

> "I don't have time to stay up all night worrying about what someone who doesn't love me has to say about me."

5. Never meditate on the criticisms of your haters.

As an actress, Viola is used to getting criticized. Sure, she might be the most decorated African American actress of all time, but that doesn't mean she doesn't have haters.

For example, critics thought she was "ugly," "fat," and "unnoteworthy," and as a result she used to be really bothered by it. However, as she reflected on the harsh pettiness of her haters, she realized she didn't really need to try to please them—or even give them a second thought. And she realized this because her haters were never going to pay her bills, love her family, or give to her what her loved ones could give to her—so she just dismissed them.

For you and me, we can learn the same lesson by realizing that the people who criticize us are not adding any real value to our lives. And anything that doesn't add value or help us, we should stop paying attention to.

SUMMARY: LIFE LESSONS FROM VIOLA DAVIS

- Your journey to greatness always involves others.
- Do everything with class.
- The best reward is recognizing how special you truly are.
- Tell the truth to the world; it needs it.
- Ignore the criticism of haters.

"I'm in control of my life, not **anyone** in Hollywood."

—Heath Ledger

CHAPTER 17

HEATH LEDGER

Heath Ledger appeared in more than 40 films in his brilliant but tragically short life. His role as Joker in *The Dark Knight* made him iconic, and his posthumous Golden Globe and Academy Award for it cemented him as a legend.

Heath was the son of a race car driver and public school teacher, and his first role as a kid was playing *Peter Pan* in Australia in a play. But it wasn't until he starred in the hit film *10 Things I Hate About You* that he became a bona fide star.

Heath then used his success in the movie to get roles in films like *The Patriot* and *Monster's Ball*, where he started to position himself to one day become a director. However, after complaining of not feeling well on the set of *The Imaginarium of Doctor Parnassus*, Heath took a few too many medications and died from an accidental overdose at the age of 28.

Nevertheless, Heath's brief life was a testament that you can still gain and share amazing wisdom and life insights no matter how old—or young—you are. And we are better off because of it because Heath shared all of himself with us.

HEATH LEDGER'S TOP LIFE LESSONS

> "I feel like I'm wasting time if I repeat myself."

1. Life only gets interesting if you try new things.

   Although Heath's stardom occurred just as Hollywood sequels and remakes were becoming a major trend, he notably never acted in one. Instead, Heath tried new projects and new roles no matter how unusual or controversial.

   For example, he acted in films that let him express everything from teen love (*10 Things I Hate About You*) to forbidden love (*Brokeback Mountain*), from courage (*The Patriot*) to psychosis (*The Dark Knight*). And he did it all while he resisted his manager's advice who tried to pigeonhole him into acting in only specific kinds of movies (to brand him to make more money).

   The lesson we can learn from this is that it is okay for us to try new things—whether it is new clothes or hairdos or jobs or careers or adventures. And we should be open to explore these new things to see what type of people we might grow into once we do.

> "If you are just safe about the choices you make, you won't grow."

2. Rewards only flow to individuals who reach for them.

One of the most difficult roles Heath ever played was as Batman's chief nemesis, Joker, in *The Dark Knight*. In the film, he had to portray a suicidal mass murderer hell bent on destroying a city— which was the exact opposite of Heath's personality as a down-to-earth and peaceful guy.

But Heath still felt the intense emotions of the Joker character not only when he was on set, but also when he was off set. For example, he famously was only able to sleep 2 hours a night when he was filming because he got wrapped up so much in the character, which he believed helped him grow into a better and stronger actor (which the Academy of Motion Picture Arts & Sciences validated when it awarded him its highest award for Best Supporting Actor).

For you and me, what we can take away is that personal and professional growth, rewards, and accomplishments will require us to push ourselves beyond our limits at times. If we don't back away from putting in the work, we can not only wow ourselves but we can wow many others who will see the fruits of our dedication.

> **"I completely live in the now, not in the past, not in the future."**

3. Being present eliminates the distractions of tomorrow and yesterday.

   The thing that Heath wanted to be more than even a movie star was a dad. And when he had a child with fellow actress Michelle Williams, his dream came true.

   Heath loved being a dad so much that when he finished on set, for example, he would rush to his car and remove his own makeup just so that he could go home to see his little girl more quickly. For Heath, family meant everything because he wanted to enjoy seeing his daughter grow up. In other words, he wanted to live in and experience those precious moments watching as she said her first words, took her first steps, and became a young lady.

   But he also wanted to experience the other precious moments life had to offer too. So as a rule, Heath tried to soak in as much as he could during each day in every area of his life so he could enjoy himself (he even famously refused to keep a daily planner because he just wanted to feel "free" in the now).

   What we can glean from this is that we should savor not only the big moments in life, but also the little ones too. For it will be in these little moments that we truly learn to live.

> "Never give up on what makes you smile."

4. If you settle for average, your soul will never leap with joy.

Heath never thought of himself as a particularly good or talented actor. But he did think of himself as somebody who loved acting and who wanted to get better at it throughout his life.

This love of acting caused Heath to leave his home in Australia and move thousands of miles away to Los Angeles because he knew acting was the only profession that could put—and keep—a smile on his face.

The lesson here is that even if our dream seems impossible, impractical, or illogical, if it is the only thing that we think of—and the only thing that really excites us—we should pursue it with all of our vigor because we will never regret chasing the thing that makes us beam from the inside.

> "As long as you have a clear picture of the life you want to lead, eventually you'll get there."

5. Once you decide on a destination, your mind figures out a roadmap to get there.

Despite being somebody who didn't keep a schedule and felt unprepared for fame, Heath knew he only wanted to be an actor. And he knew he wanted to be an actor not for the fame of it, but for the experience of making films.

For example, Heath truly enjoyed being on set and embodying new characters because he found it fascinating learning about different types of people and personality types and portraying them in front of the camera. But he didn't do this because he was thinking about the red carpet; he did this because this is what he always imagined his life would be like while running after his dream of acting in Hollywood.

In our own lives, if we decide on what we want to do—and who we want to be—we can make consistent decisions that align our reality with our dreams.

SUMMARY: LIFE LESSONS FROM HEATH LEDGER

- You must try new things to keep life interesting.
- Your rewards will only come if you reach for them.
- Stop focusing on the distractions of tomorrow and yesterday; focus on today.
- Settling for average will steal your joy.
- Your mind will naturally plot the way for your desired destination in life.

"You're not a star until they can spell your name in Karachi."

—Humphrey Bogart

CHAPTER 18

HUMPHREY BOGART

Humphrey Bogart is considered by many to be the greatest American film actor to ever live. He was a member of the famous Rat Pack—with Frank Sinatra—and starred in beloved films ranging from Casablanca to Dark Passages, The Maltese Falcon to The African Queen (for which he won the Academy Award for Best Actor).

But before becoming a Hollywood star, Humphrey was kicked out of school for throwing a teacher in the pond and for generally being rebellious. However, this all changed when he entered the Navy to serve during World War 1, where he became a studious and disciplined young man.

After he returned from the service, Humphrey began his entertainment career on Broadway - where he would star in dozens of plays throughout the course of his lifetime—before becoming the king of gangster films in the 1930s and 1940s in Tinseltown.

HUMPHREY BOGART'S LIFE LESSONS

> "I always cry at weddings, especially my own."

1. It's okay to laugh at yourself.

   Although Humphrey was married 4 times, he never failed to laugh at his own shortcomings in relationships - or in any area of life. For example, Humphrey would jokingly name nice items he bought after at least one of his wives (Mayo Method) to remember them.

   But Humphrey would also laugh at his looks and acting talent too. He didn't believe, for example, that he was as handsome as other actors, or as talented as them either. And he was completely fine with this, as he embraced who he was without getting bent out of shape based on things he thought he might lack in comparison to others.

   The lesson we can learn from this is that even if we are brave enough to see ourselves and our inconsistencies honestly like Humphrey, we don't have to draw negative conclusions about our self-worth. Instead, we can see that we are human just like everyone else and laugh at our own misgivings.

> "Everybody has something to conceal."

2. Nobody is as they appear.

More than anything else, Humphrey despised people who were arrogant and fake. In fact, he would speak publicly about the "pretenders" he saw all around him in Hollywood—which didn't win him many friends.

For example, Humphrey was not very popular in Tinseltown because he would criticize directors or producers, not out of spite but out of honesty (if they were not behaving appropriately). Even though this caused the most popular actors of the day to avoid him - and the studios to try to control his public persona—it nevertheless won him affection with the press because Humphrey wasn't willing to keep private his own thoughts or keep private the open secrets in Hollywood that the industry was trying to bury to make money.

What we can take away from this is that even if others try to get us to hide things to preserve an image, we don't have to go along with their plans just because it benefits them or their financial bottom lines. Instead, we can be honest and understand that some people are trying to cover things up and if these cover ups hurt others, we can speak our minds about it even if others disagree with or try to stop us.

> "There is more to talking than just words."

3. You must master how to talk with your body.

One of the benefits to starting his career in show business on Broadway was that Humphrey was able to learn how to use his body to communicate with others. For example, in his plays *Nerves* and *Meet the Wife*, he was able to truly take control of his body language to speak without having to utter words.

Humphrey also applied these same lessons to his films in Hollywood like *Bad Sister*, *Petrified Forest*, and many others so that he could let others completely understand and "feel" what he was thinking through body language alone.

In our own lives, when we learn how to talk with our eyes, with our hands, with our posture, and with our bodies in other ways, we can begin to see that speaking involves more than stringing together words. In fact, we can begin to see that we can be even more powerful—and effective—speakers when we do this than just by simply talking.

> "The way to survive an Oscar is never to try to win another one."

4. Life is about more than trophies and awards.

Humphrey was nominated for an Oscar for his performance in Casablanca and won his first one for his performance in *The African Queen*. But despite Hollywood swooning over his acting talent, Humphrey didn't feel the pressure—or desire—to make movies just to be crowned the king of the Academy Awards (or any other awards).

For example, Humphrey strongly believed that many actors would become more fearful after they were nominated for or won an Oscar. And be believed this because the subsequent work they chose—and the performances they delivered—seemed to be much safer and less bold than their prior work.

As a consequence of this belief, Humphrey didn't want to become static and stale and play it safe like others just so that he could win awards. Instead, he wanted to become bolder and more adventurous in his acting choices so that he could stretch himself (even if the award voters did not understand what he was doing and would choose to never again nominate him).

For you and me, we can see that living for awards—or for material success—can cause us to drift from what is in our hearts to do. If we choose not to make our lives (or careers) about the outward rewards that we can get—and instead choose to make them about how much we can give of ourselves by stretching and growing with each new role, project, and opportunity—we will be much more satisfied than by always playing it safe.

> "A hotdog at the game beats roast beef at the Ritz."

5. Even movie stars never outgrow the simple pleasures of life.

As mentioned, Humphrey hated anything that reeked of pretension. And this included walking the red carpet and movie premieres.

For example, Humphrey rarely would attend the premieres of his own movies. But what he would do instead is have his publicist issue a press release as to why he couldn't be there so that he could avoid mingling—and keep the public happy.

What we can learn from this is that the trappings of our jobs or lives—the money, the lights, the admiration—do not have to become our reason for why we do what we do. Even if we don't go as far as Humphrey in terms of avoiding the applause of others, we can still realize that there can be just as much joy in living away from the limelight as there is living in it.

SUMMARY: LIFE LESSONS FROM HUMPREY BOGART

- The greatest people in the world learn to laugh at themselves.
- Appearances can be deceiving, for everyone.
- Master how you talk with your body.
- Know that there is more to life than awards and trophies.
- Seek to always enjoy the simple pleasures of life.

"I'm a strong person with or without this person, with or without this job, and with or without these tight pants."

—Queen Latifah

CHAPTER 19

QUEEN LATIFAH

Queen Latifah is an Emmy, Grammy, and Golden Globe winner who has not only starred in her own successful sitcom, but who has also hosted her own successful talk show during a time few Black women were ever given the chance to. She has appeared in numerous films including *Set it Off, Girls Trip, 22 Jump Street*, and *Ice Age*. And she has sold millions of albums as one of the first female rappers to reach mainstream success in America.

Queen Latifah began her career as a teenager beat boxing for the all-female hip hop troupe, Ladies Fresh Group, and frequently crosses musical boundaries as her octave range enables her to both rap and sing. Her artistic work often includes social empowerment issues, and she is considered the Queen of Jazz-Rap, and her artistic skills are some of the most unique in history.

QUEEN LATIFAH'S TOP 5 LIFE LESSONS

> "Life is much bigger, grander, higher, and wider than we allow ourselves to think. We're capable of so much more than we allow ourselves to believe."

1. Magic exists if only you will search for it.

   Although Queen Latifah came from a good family—her mom is a teacher and her dad is a police officer—she still didn't grow up with exposure to the kind of artists she dreamt of becoming. But despite her lack of exposure, she decided to put herself in position to be around other artists even though they weren't world famous superstars. And she did this by acting in school musicals and joining local singing groups, which is what made all of the difference for her.

   For example, Queen Latifah was able to leverage her exposure to local artists to learn from them so she could take what she learned to go to higher and higher levels, both artistically and professionally. So, by the time she joined the Ladies Fresh Group and Flavor Unit, she had learned and sharpened her skills enough to put together her own rap recording, which led to her first single "Wrath of My Madness."

   The lesson for us here is that our dreams—and the world—are so much bigger than the day-to-day reality that we live in. But if we want to experience more of our dreams and our world, we will have to put ourselves in the position to by initially taking baby steps to surround ourselves with people who are doing what we want to do (even if it is initially on a very small and local level).

> "Most people don't have so much talent that they can become a success all their own. We all need people to help us and lift us up."

2. Your success depends not only on your hard work, but on other people helping you along the way.

Queen Latifah believes that one of the most ironic things about being an artist who puts out individual work is that that work cannot be seen without the help and support of many other people. And she is right. In her own life, for example, it took being discovered by Dante Ross and Fab 5 Freddy—the host of Yo! MTV Rap—before she could release her debut album, *All Hail The Queen*.

But being discovered once and releasing an inaugural album still wasn't enough for Queen Latifah to reach the kind of mainstream success that she would need to become an icon. She recognized that she would have to continue working with—and being helped by—more and more people if she wanted to become a Grammy winner and grow into the best possible artist she was capable of. (Of course, she did become a Grammy winner with the song U.N.I.T.Y. but only after being supported by many other people who she convinced to believe in her.)

What we can learn from her is that even if we're smart and work hard, we still have to be helped by others to achieve our goals and the kind of success we want with our lives. Yes, we will put ourselves in a better position to reach our dreams when we are shrewd and diligent, but we still have to learn how to get along with and be supported by others along the way.

> "When I was around 18, I looked in the mirror and said, 'You're either going to love yourself or hate yourself.' And I decided to love myself. That changed a lot of things."

3. The number 1 secret to self-care is liking and respecting the person staring back at you in the mirror.

When somebody looks at Queen Latifah, it might be easy for them to assume that she was destined not only for stardom, but that she was endowed with an other-worldly self-confidence and self-love that made it easy for her to be resilient and become the icon that she is. But if you speak with her, you will realize that it wasn't her "destiny" that allowed her to become the person she is today: it was her decision.

When Queen Latifah was just a teenager, for example, she decided to accept every part of herself—she accepted that she was a 5 foot 10 inch, Black female rapper from Jersey who would get questioned for everything from jumping into a male-dominated music scene to her own sexuality. And she was ok with that.

For you and me, one of the biggest lessons in life we should learn is that self-love and self-care is a conscious choice of accepting who we are without complaints. And learning to accept ourselves without being dismissive of our true strengths and treasures (even if these strengths and treasures are buried deeply within or been overlooked by others).

> "I decided early on that I was going to put on my crown and rule my world by acting right and treating myself like a queen."

4. Becoming the best version of yourself begins by acting like the best version of yourself.

Queen Latifah is one of the most underrated legends in Hollywood because she has not tried to convince anyone of her greatness. She knew she was great and that, eventually, that greatness would be shown to others if she simply walked, talked, and lived as the person she believed herself to be.

For example, although there had never been a rapper to perform at a Superbowl prior to her— and although there had never been a Black woman to cross musical and acting genres like her before— Queen Latifah knew early on she could reach the epitome of artistic success by treating herself like the artistic success she would eventually become.

The takeaway here is that it is not only OK to act like you have already achieved your goals or manifested your greatness prior to doing so, but it is absolutely essential to. It is essential because the person we think we are will eventually become the person that we actually are, so we should act like that great person before we one day become that great person.

> "How many crossroads are you allowed to have in life? I seem to have a lot of crossroads. I think maybe I crossed back across the same road too often."

5. The quality of your life depends on the choices you make over and over again.

Like other icons, Queen Latifah has had to bear her own crosses several times in life. For example, she had a very public battle with Foxy Brown that resulted in both putting out 'dis' albums against one another that were both embarrassing and hurtful.

But after this feud went on for several years, Queen Latifah realized that it was better to take the high road and reconcile with Foxy Brown than to continue holding a grudge and acting in ways that were inconsistent with the kind of peace-loving and kind person that she is.

In our own lives, we can learn that many of the crossroads we will face in life will be ones where we have to not only forgive others who have hurt us, but ones where we will have to ask for forgiveness from those we have hurt.

SUMMARY: LIFE LESSONS FROM QUEEN LATIFAH

- Search for magic and you will find it.
- Success depends on your own hard work AND help from others.
- The best self-care is loving and respecting yourself.
- Act like the best version of yourself and you will become the best version of yourself.
- The quality of your choices will determine the quality of your life.

"Do not bring me small ideas; bring me big ideas."

—Arnold Schwarzenegger

CHAPTER 20

QUEEN LATIFAH

Arnold Schwarzenegger is a former Mr. Universe, 7 x Mr. Olympia, and New York Times bestselling author of the book "Total Recall." As the star of the beloved *Terminator* and *Conan the Barbarian* series, Arnold has etched out a place for himself in Hollywood history as one of the most iconic personalities ever to grace Tinseltown.

Although Arnold has succeeded at every dream he ever put his mind to—he is, for example, the former Governor of California and has an estimated net worth more than $100 million dollars— his childhood was anything less than ideal. For example, his parents were very strict and his father even severely abused him growing up. Nevertheless, Arnold was able to take his childhood pain and channel it into a desire to escape his circumstances that would one day turn him into a legend.

ARNOLD SCHWARZENEGGER'S TOP 5 LIFE LESSONS

> "The worst thing I can be is the same as everybody else. I hate that."

1. If two people are the same, one of them is unnecessary—don't let it be you.

After Arnold succeeded as a bodybuilder in the Mr. Universe and Olympia competitions, he came to Hollywood where every producer told him he was "too muscular" to be a star. At the time, for example, skinnier and shorter men were getting top billing in movies and anybody who didn't fit that norm was immediately dismissed.

However, Arnold rejected the idea that he had to slim down or not appear as big in order to be cast. Instead, he emphasized his unique qualities—namely, his huge muscles and near-perfect physique—to get roles in films like *Conan the Barbarian* and *Terminator* that could only go to somebody his size. In other words, instead of bending who he was to fit Hollywood's fleeting expectations, Arnold made Hollywood bend to him. And it worked.

In our own lives, we should realize that just because everybody else might be the same (i.e., they might think the same or look the same, etc.) doesn't mean we have to. Often when we try to be like others, we blend in and become an echo and never really develop the unusual or unique aspects of ourselves that will allow us to stand out and prosper.

> **"Being surrounded by winners helps you develop into a winner."**

2. Success can be predicted by who you hang out with.

Whether Arnold was competing in bodybuilding, acting in Hollywood, or being political as Governor of California, he only had one rule: to surround himself with the best people in the fields he wanted to conquer at the time.

For example, Arnold became friends and workout partners with Lou Ferrigno who was himself a Mr. Olympia and Hollywood actor (he was the star of the *Incredible Hulk* in the 1970s). Arnold also did the same thing when he married into the famed Kennedy family before entering into politics—he wanted to be amongst the brightest minds in government in America. And he did this because he knew that not only could he get more opportunities by running with winners, but that he could become even more of a winner with others than he could on his own.

The lesson we can learn from this is that the environment we voluntarily choose to place ourselves in can be as important—if not more important—a predictor of our success than anything else. So, if we want to succeed and be winners, we will have to personally and professionally only associate with successful winners (and we will, unfortunately, have to remove ourselves from anyone or anything that doesn't have that mindset).

> "Don't go where it's crowded. Go where it's empty. Even though it's harder to get there, that's where you belong and that's where there's less competition."

3. Pick a narrow niche and become the best in the world at it.

One of the most important secrets of success is learning to dominate a niche field or area. And Arnold learned this early on. For example, he dedicated himself at 15 to bodybuilding (a field few were in) and then to being a buff action star (also something uncommon in the 1970s and 1980s) so that he would have little competition in reaching his goals.

But he also did this in politics. When he was running for governor, for example, he did it during a once-in-a-lifetime recall where he did not have to run against many other candidates in a crowded primary field (that would have dramatically lowered his odds of winning). Instead, he skipped that process entirely and ran directly against the then-governor who was being recalled so that he wouldn't have to compete against so many people.

The takeaway is that if we decide to narrow our focus like Arnold so that we don't have as much competition in our quest to reach our goals, not only can we more likely reach them but we can also reach them more quickly.

> **"You have to remember something: everybody pities the weak. Jealousy has to be earned."**

4. If you have no haters, you haven't reached the peak of your greatness yet.

Sometimes it is easy to forget that a legend like Arnold has had many critics. But he has, and they were legion.

For example, when Arnold first became an actor, critics lambasted his Austrian accent as it was difficult to understand him at the time. In fact, producers and studio executives even wanted him to get a voice coach to get rid of his unique style of speech. But Arnold refused and his refusal is what led to famous lines like "I'll be back" in Terminator that allowed him to become a global phenomenon.

Even though some critics and executives hated how he spoke—and were jealous of the success he gained because he refused to bend over for them—Arnold knew his greatness could only be found in his own uniqueness even if that uniqueness was guaranteed to breed haters.

For you and me, having haters is a sign that we are on the right track because, as Arnold said, "jealousy has to be earned." And jealousy is only earned through success, uniqueness, or greatness.

> "You'll get more from being a peacemaker than a warrior."

5. The most successful people on earth know how to get along with others.

When Arnold became Governor of California, he was successful in passing numerous reforms in the first few months of his term. However, it was when he decided to declare war on the teachers union and nurses union—simultaneously—that he suffered his biggest political defeat.

For example, Arnold attempted to bypass working with the unions by going directly to the people through multiple ballot initiatives, but he was soundly defeated. And he was defeated not because he wasn't popular with the people but because he didn't attempt to make peace and negotiate with the unions to try to get his own desired reforms.

The lesson we can learn from this is that while we do have to battle at times, in general we catch more bees with honey than we do with vinegar. In other words, we must learn to get along with people in most (but not all) circumstances if we want to reach our various goals. This means we have to learn how others think and feel, how to communicate with them with respect and honor, and how to incentivize them to see our point of view to encourage them to support us so we can more quickly or easily reach our goals.

SUMMARY: LIFE LESSONS FROM ARNOLD SCHWARENEGGER

- Don't become irrelevant by being the same as everyone else.
- The circle you hang within determines your level of success.
- Become the best at the niche of your choosing.
- One prerequisite to greatness is being poked by a nest of haters.
- Cultivate success by getting along with others.

"I am the me I chose to be."

—Sidney Poitier

CHAPTER 21

SIDNEY POITIER

Sidney Poitier was the first Black male to win an Academy Award and one of the first Black males to win a Grammy Award for best spoken word album. As an actor and director, his life's work was history-defining and has helped pave the way for equality in the United States (and around the world).

Sidney was the youngest son of 7 children and had to work in jobs ranging from being a dishwasher to treating psychiatric patients, and he used his difficult experiences to shape the empathy he brought to his acting roles. And we are all better off because of it.

SIDNEY POITIER'S TOP 5 LIFE LESSONS

> "I had chosen to use my work as a reflection of my values."

1. Never divorce what you do from who you are.

   Throughout Sidney's entire career, he was often the only Black person working on set—in front of the camera or behind it. And he was often the only Black person on set even on socially conscious films.

   For example, when he starred in the film *Guess Who's Coming To Dinner*—about interracial marriage (and equality)—the set was not diverse, but he still chose to work on it because he believed the content of the movie could help change America. And it did. (The film was a precursor to *Loving vs. Virginia*, the U.S. Supreme Court case that outlawed the ban on interracial marriage nationwide.)

   What this can teach us is that not only should we work on projects we believe in that reflect our values, but we should do it even if the circumstances aren't perfect. Even though Sidney didn't have equality on set, for example, he knew he could sacrifice that if it meant helping to bring equality everywhere off set. We should do the same.

> "I have always been a learner because I knew nothing."

2. Accepting that you need to learn more than you currently do is the first step in becoming greater.

Sidney was a descendant of slaves who were not allowed to read, write, or integrate into society. As a consequence, he always placed a high value on learning (but not necessarily on schooling).

For example, Sidney became very interested in politics so he threw himself into the study of history so that he could be appointed as Ambassador to Japan from the Bahamas, which he was for many years. Without his desire to learn more, he could never have successfully taken on the role like he had.

For you and me, what we can learn is that no matter how skilled or successful we are, we can always become more so. Even Sidney committed himself to learning new things in his 70s and 80s just so that he could be an ambassador, and so should we. Regardless of our age or success, we should continue learning as much as we can.

> "I've learned that I have to find positive outlets for anger or it will destroy me."

3. Your emotions are only helpful when you can channel them toward something constructive.

When Sidney joined the American Negro Theater, he had the opportunity to perform for the first time for all-black audiences. But there was only one problem: they didn't like him!

Sidney was booed off stage, for example, because he couldn't sing and because he had an accent. To audiences who saw him perform, he failed to meet their basic expectations and so he was angry and dejected. But he didn't let this cause him to become bitter or quit; instead, he let it fuel his drive to get better so that one day he could become the best—in a related field (acting, as opposed to musicals) that he was more suited for.

The lesson here is that when people don't accept us for who we are, we do not need to become negative. Instead, we should use their lack of acceptance as motivation to excel in positive ways. Although this is easier said than done, Sidney believed had he not done this he would not have gone on to become the icon that he did.

> "If I'm remembered for having done a few good things, and if my presence here has sparked some good energies, that's plenty."

4. True success only comes down to a few simple things.

It is true that Sidney starred in films like *Lillies in the Field*, *A Raisin in the Sun*, and *In The Heat of the Night*, but he thought his life was so much more than these things. That is, he felt that he was more than just a man who could recite lines and win awards.

For example, Sidney believed in being a positive experience for everybody who worked with him. To him, if you were going to be in his presence you were going to benefit from it. And the benefit you experienced from it would not just be in the form of money or success: it would be in the form of laughing, smiling, and feeling appreciated because that is what Sidney would give to you.

For you and me, the more we recognize that it is the residue we plant inside of others—the hope, joy, laughter, and peace—that will make us true successes, the less we will care about likes, status, and other superficial symbols of material success.

> "The only weapon I had was to say no."

5. Your "no" can be the best choice you ever make.

As a Black man in America, Sidney was told "no" a lot. But as a Black star in Hollywood, he also had the ability to say no a lot too—and he did.

For example, he was offered numerous roles to portray Black men as criminals or imbeciles, but he turned them down because he wanted to bring dignity to his race, not just negative stereotypes. Even though this cost him some money in the short run, it earned him something even better in the long run: respect.

The lesson here is that, no matter how enticing a questionable offer we get (whether professional or personal), we always have the choice to say no to the things that could not only harm us and our reputations, but harm those who are close to us or who we represent.

SUMMARY: LIFE LESSONS FROM SIDNEY POITIER

- What you do for a living should not be divorced from who you are as a person.
- Becoming greater requires that you always learn more.
- Channel your emotions to something constructive.
- Doing a few simple things will bring success.
- One of the best choices you can make is saying "no."

"In certain moment's in our lives we get little signals, little **flashes** that say it's yours if you want it."

—Anthony Hopkins

CHAPTER 22
ANTHONY HOPKINS

Anthony Hopkins is an Academy Award winning film, television, and stage actor who trained at the Royal Academy of Dramatic Art in London. He has starred in movies including *Silence of the Lambs*, *The Elephant Man*, *Nixon*, and *Amistad*, among others. And he has toured around the world as a musical composer with multiple symphonic albums to his name.

Anthony grew up as the son of a working class baker, and was not very good academically. Instead, he turned his attention to things like drawing and painting in school which eventually led him into a career in the arts and one of the greatest careers in Hollywood history.

ANTHONY HOPKIN'S TOP 5 LIFE LESSONS

> "Once you begin to fall off the track and believe you breathe different air to everyone else, you're doomed; you're finished."

1. Arrogance will bury you.

   Although Anthony is one of the most decorated actors in history—having earned Oscars, Emmys, and Cecille B. Demille award—he nevertheless doesn't believe his own press. That is, he tries not to get caught up in the hype and attention he gets as he not only believes it is illusory, but he also dislikes it very much.

   But these aren't the only reasons why he doesn't believe in arrogance. Growing up, for example, he would look at his fathers hardened hands—from doing so much baking as a baker—and he realized that it's the hardworking everyday people who make the world go round, not the hot shot celebrities. This early experience instilled inside of him a deep belief that he should never think of himself as better than anyone else regardless of how successful he became.

   The takeaway here is that even if we have money, power, status, and everything that goes along with it, we should never let it go to our heads. If one of the most famous and successful people in the world like Anthony doesn't, we shouldn't either. Because if we do, it will not only cause us to begin looking down on others, but it will cause us to think we are invincible—the one belief that has destroyed 100% of people who have held it.

> **"Beware of the tyranny of the weak. They just suck you dry."**

2. The bigger you become, the more others will think you owe them something.

   Throughout his career, Anthony has earned a lot of money which has not only changed his tax bracket, but also his relationships. For example, many of the people he now associates with happen to be well off like himself because his excellence has paid the price for his admission to a new social circle.

   But not everybody thinks they need to pay the same price to this circle as him. Instead, they feel entitled that Anthony should give them money or open doors—or do any number of other things—just because he has worked hard to be successful. However, Anthony thinks that there are limits to what he can do because, in his experience, many people will try to latch on to his success to advance themselves without putting in the blood, sweat, and tears for their own success.

   The lesson we can learn from this is that there will always be others around us who want to take advantage of what we can do for them. This doesn't mean we should be cynical or not help them; it simply means that we must learn to recognize who only wants to take from us (and not give to us) and separate ourselves from them. And we should learn to separate ourselves quickly.

> "Today is the tomorrow I was worried about yesterday."

3. Living too much in the past or future brings unnecessary anxiety.

As Anthony has aged, he has been able to see it all in life. And he's been able to experience it all too.

For example, not only has he worked with superstar directors like Steven Spielberg (on films like *Amistad*), but he has also worked with some not so stellar directors. Some of these less than A-list filmmakers have been so full of anxiety and control issues—because they were so full of fear about what "might happen"—Anthony has refused to work with them (he has literally walked off set if they could not get themselves together).

For you and me, we can see that even though it is easy to be anxious about certain things—and even though we might try to control certain things—this is no way to live life. Not only will others pick up on this if we do this, but they will be turned off by it too. The only way to avoid worrying about things is to literally stop worrying about them. We must choose to live in the present and not project our fears onto others.

> "I would hope not to be so arrogant as to doubt anybody's religion or belief."

4. Respecting others' beliefs is not the same as agreeing with them.

At one point in his life, Anthony was agnostic and wasn't sure how others could believe things contrary to his agnosticism. That is, he didn't know whether he believed in God and how others could so strongly believe in God. After all, wouldn't those who disagree with him just be stupid or evil for believing what they did?

But over time, Anthony started to think differently. He no longer considers himself an agnostic and believes that he is only but a small microbe in the vastness of the universe controlled by a God who has been very good to him. And he believes that others can sincerely reach different conclusions than us without us arrogantly trying to pigeonhole or ridicule them.

The takeaway from this is that on important issues in our personal and professional lives—whether they be religious, political, cultural, or economic—we should not bully people into agreeing with us. And we should not dismiss them either. Instead, we should learn where they're coming from and, if we still disagree with them, simply accept that they have the right to feel how they want to without us trying to make them into our own image.

> "Life's too short to deal with other people's insecurities."

5. Do not spend time with people who have no control over themselves.

Anthony famously was the understudy of Sir Lawrence Olivier, the great British actor who dominated much of European and American cinema in the 20th Century. And as his understudy, he learned that there would always be other people around him—actors, audiences, and the like—who would bring their insecurities to him. But Lawrence told him that he had to dismiss these things because life was too short to be focused on playing up to (or accommodating) people's worries and fears.

What we can learn from this is that even though we should love, help, and encourage others, we do not have to endlessly subject ourselves to their insecurities. That is, we don't have to allow ourselves to be their emotional doormats if they cannot learn to heal themselves; we simply can only do so much for others and might have to love them from a distance if they refuse to change.

SUMMARY: LIFE LESSONS FROM ANTHONY HOPKINS

- Don't let arrogance destroy you.
- Others will think you owe them something when you start to rise to the top.
- Eliminate unnecessary anxiety; live in the present.
- You can respect other people's beliefs without agreeing with them.
- Keep a distance from people who lack self-control.

"Love has nothing to do with what you are expecting to get, only with what you are expecting to give."

—Katharine Hepburn

CHAPTER 23
KATHARINE HEPBURN

Katharine Hepburn is considered by many to be the greatest actress of the classic era in Hollywood. Not only did she win 4 Academy Awards for Best Actress, but she broke racial barriers during the height of America's mistreatment of Black people.

For example, though Katharine was a White woman, she appeared in the groundbreaking film *Guess Who's Coming To Dinner?*, which many consider to be the film that paved the way for interracial marriage to be legalized by the Supreme Court in the United States.

But Katharine also shunned other prejudices of the day too. In her wardrobe, for example, she refused to wear dresses because wearing pants was more comfortable for her (which seems like a minor thing now but back then it was a major controversy).

In all, Katharine appeared in nearly 50 films, multiple television movies, and over 30 stage plays and is the epitome of the quixotic movie star who lived life on her own terms.

KATHARINE HEPBURN'S TOP LIFE LESSONS

> "If you obey all the rules you miss all the fun."

1. Only those that challenge the status quo are remembered by history.

   Katharine came to fame during a time when women were supposed to stay home, raise children, and submit to their husbands without question. But to Katharine, this was not to be her life.

   For example, she was raised by strong parents who taught her not to conform to public opinion or popular pressure just because everyone believed or did a certain thing. For example, not only did she wear pants publicly, but she was also athletic and played sports all of her life—hardly something anyone thought a glamorous movie star should be doing. And as a consequence, she became deeply unpopular during her time—but especially beloved by history for taking a strong stand for what she believed in.

   What we can learn from this is we can live life on our own terms so that we can enjoy who we are. And even if those around us don't understand it, it doesn't matter because we will still be having fun—and may even be remembered by others for being truly iconoclastic.

> "It would be a terrific innovation if you could get your mind to stretch a little further than the next wisecrack."

2. The most intelligent minds cultivate a long-term perspective.

Katharine brought an elegance and sophistication to her role as movie star. But even though she played strong-willed women and in dramatic roles, she was also known to enjoy performing in comedies.

For example, she starred in *Bringing Up Baby* and *Holiday* with Cary Grant, *Woman of the Year*, and *Adam's Rib*, which was named by the American Film Institute as one of the greatest comedies of all time. So, to Katharine, having a good laugh was always something she welcomed.

However, Katharine never believed that having a good laugh was the only thing that people should be having. Nor did she believe that being a smart aleck was the best approach to life, as it often discounted taking the long-term view. Instead, she believed that people should practice being both joyful and substantive, both joke-y and wise. In other words, she believed that people should use humor to get through the tough moments of life but also wisdom to see the long-term perspective so that they could have something to look forward to.

In our own lives, embracing both laughter and wisdom will help us power through any season of life we find ourselves in.

> "I don't care what is written about me so long as it isn't true."

3. Your personal privacy is nobody else's business.

Part of the reason Katharine was named "the greatest American [female] screen legend" and one of the 100 most important women of the 20th Century is because in addition to being talented, she was notoriously mysterious. For example, she very rarely gave interviews about herself or personal life and did not believe it was a good business strategy to do so.

One particular example of this is when a member of the press asked her if she had any children and she said, "yes, I have five: two white and three colored." This was at a time when interracial marriage was forbidden by law and even more forbidden by society. But to Katharine, she did not think it was the press's business to know about her family life so she let them speculate about her home life based on her bold statements.

What we can learn from this is that, even though we live in an era where some have declared that privacy is dead, we do not have to reveal all aspects of our lives to others just because they want us to. Katharine believed that cultivating a bit of mystery about herself was smart—and it paid off for her in terms of keeping rampant speculation and interest in her career alive. This lesson can also pay off for us if we choose to embrace more mystique in our lives and careers.

> "The time to make up your mind about people is never."

4. Very little is accomplished when you jump to conclusions about others.

Although Katharine was very bold about her political beliefs—her views prompted picketing of some of her movies, for example—she still believed that people were a work in progress. As such, she didn't think that drawing conclusions about people—good or bad—was the wisest thing to do (even if those people opposed her).

In our own lives, we should understand the same thing: that jumping to conclusions about others—or believing others cannot change—will not do us very much good. Instead, we should understand that people are still developing all throughout their lives (regardless of their age) so we should always keep that in mind when forming opinions about them.

> "Life is full of censorship."

5. History is rarely made by those who censor themselves or play it safe.

As mentioned, many people tried to censor Katharine throughout her life. Whether it be because she wore pants and was athletic, or because she supported interracial marriage, people rose up against her and tried to impose their beliefs onto all she said and did. But to no avail.

Katharine remained fiercely outspoken and independent throughout her 96 years of life because she felt it was the right thing to do. Even though this made her unpopular at the time, she is now looked back on with fondness for her bold determination and grace to withstand the censorship others tried to put her through.

What we can learn from this is that our voices matter, our opinions matter, our perspectives matter, and that we matter. Even if some in society do not believe that—and even if some in society try to cancel or censor us—we should continue standing for what is right and let history be our vindicator.

SUMMARY: LIFE LESSONS FROM KATHARINE KEPBURN

- You must challenge the the status quo of your generation to be remembered by the history books.
- Cultivating a long-term perspective is a sign of the most intelligent minds.
- No one owns your personal privacy but you.
- Jumping to conclusions does not accomplish much.
- Censoring yourself, or playing it safe, is not the path to making history.

"No, I don't see many movies. I don't even see my own movies."

—Michael Keaton

CHAPTER 24
MICHAEL KEATON

Michael Keaton is a Golden Globe winning actor and comedian with a 40+ year career in Hollywood. He is best known for his roles in *Beetlejuice*, *Spiderman*, *Birdman*, and, of course, *Batman* and *Batman Returns*.

Michael grew up in Pittsburg and began his career in local plays and television there. Most famously, he was cast to play the Flying Zookeeni Brothers in *Mister Rogers Neighborhood* which was filmed near where he grew up.

MICHAEL KEATON'S TOP 5 LIFE LESSONS

> "Dying is a really hard way to learn about life."

1. Begin regularly reflecting on life lessons to reduce the number of future regrets.

Michael was fortunate that one of his early experiences was on the set of *Mister Rogers Neighborhood* because it instilled inside of him a focus on the things that matter. That is, the show focused on good vs. bad behavior, right vs. wrong, and top lessons in life for children. But Michael was also able to apply what he learned on the show to his own life.

As a consequence of this formative experience, Michael began to see that in taking on roles in Hollywood it wasn't just about the end result with them (i.e., critical or commercial success, stardom, etc). He began to see that it was more about who he spent time with, what he learned, and how much of a good time that he had. To him, this became a guiding principle in his career and life that allowed him to put things into perspective and not get caught up in the ego and superfluous drama of Tinseltown.

The lesson that can be learned from this is that, no matter what your profession or goal, you should be regularly reflecting on the daily experience you are having in pursuit of whatever it is that you're looking for. The more you reflect—on what you're learning, the good and the bad of your experience, and how you can improve your soul (and not just reach your goal)—the wiser you'll become on your path (and the more peaceful, happy, and successful you will become too).

> "There comes a point in your life when you realize how quickly time goes by, and how quickly it has gone. Then it really speeds up exponentially."

2. You may only have 30,000-40,000 days on the earth, so use them wisely.

For many people, the last they saw of Michael Keaton was in his role playing Bruce Wayne in *Batman* and *Batman Returns* before they saw him roar back in *Birdman*—nearly 25 years later. But the question is, what did Michael Keaton do during all of the intervening years? The answer: he lived life.

For Michael even though he was still acting in movies and experiencing life, time flew by. And for him, this was a huge surprise because he didn't realize life would be as fast as it was. It was literally like he blinked and decades passed.

What you and I can learn about this is that the older we get, the more time speeds up. As children, we think we have all of the time in the world but as we become more mature we realize we have to begin to count our days as they go by in the blink of an eye. For most people, they will live around 30,000 days on the earth (80 years) before they pass on to the next adventure, so savoring each one will be a very important lesson to learn and apply.

> "I never saw what I do for a living as who I am."

3. Your work, success, and accomplishments are not your identity.

Although Michael became one of the biggest stars in Hollywood, he never let that go to his head. In fact, he refused to even live in Los Angeles long-term in favor of residing in his native Pittsburg.

Part of the reason Michael did this was because he was more comfortable living near where he grew up—like most people. But another part of the reason is because he recognized that being an actor and movie star was his title, not his identity. And as a result, he saw his work as just that: work.

The takeaway from this is that the more we allow our work and success to define who we are, the more at-risk we will be for arrogance, shallowness, and missing the special moments life has to offer. Instead, we should be proud of our work, but also not allow it to determine our self-worth because if our work or success ever goes, so does our soul. And we don't need to put that much pressure on ourselves.

> "I'm just shocked at how blatantly shallow people are sometimes."

4. Most people won't ever try to know the real you.

One of the greatest characters Michael played was a former superhero actor who was washed up in the movie *Birdman*. Of course, it was a meta-reflection on how people perceived his real-life career which was simultaneously funny and insulting.

It was funny because Michael had a sense of humor about the ups and downs of Hollywood—and how people thought he might have been washed up. It was insulting because even though Michael had not been in a breakout role for nearly 25 years, he was still a human being with dignity and worth and felt he shouldn't be defined by whether he had superstar status or not in the eyes of others.

The life lesson is that people are going to form opinions about you whether they actually know the real you or not. And the more known you are, the stronger their opinions—and judgments—about you will be, but you have to learn to dismiss it as most of their thoughts have nothing to do with the real you (only with the superficial you they have constructed in their heads).

> "I choose not to be at the whim of others. I want to be at my own whim."

5. If you don't decide what your schedule will be, others will.

Michael was directed by iconic filmmaker Tim Burton in *Batman* and *Batman Returns*. But when Tim left the franchise—both he and Michael were slated to reprise their roles in *Batman 3*—Michael left too.

Although Michael met the new director of *Batman 3* and was offered $15 million for the role, he turned it down because he wanted to call his own shots in life. He wanted to work with his preferred director, for example, and make a different kind of movie and, when he couldn't, he walked.

The takeaway here is not that we should never compromise if we don't get everything we want. The takeaway is that life is too short to not live it (mostly) on your own terms. You should put yourself in a position where you can regularly do so (even if you can't in every single circumstance).

SUMMARY: LIFE LESSONS FROM MICHAEL KEATON

- Reduce future regrets by regularly reflecting on the choices you're making in life.
- Use your days on earth wisely.
- Your identity as a human being is greater than your accomplishments, success, and work.
- Few people will get to know the real you.
- Decide how you will schedule your life before others do it for you.

"Just standing around looking beautiful is so boring."

—Michelle Pfeiffer

CHAPTER 25

MICHELLE PFIEFER

Michelle Pfeiffer is an Emmy and Oscar nominated actress from Orange County, California who got her breakthrough role starring in *Grease* 2 at just 23 years old. Since then, she has played in iconic films ranging from *Scarface* to *Batman Returns* to *Dangerous Minds* and beyond.

Growing up, she was the daughter of an air-condition contractor and served as a checkout girl at the supermarket chain Vons. She trained to be a court stenographer but quickly transitioned to acting even though she had no formal training in it. She is considered one of the most beautiful and successful actresses of all time.

> "You have no idea what it's like to be famous until you become famous."

1. **Imagining something is different than experiencing it.**

   Although Michelle won the starring role in Grease 2 because of her quirkiness, she didn't become a household name until years later. In fact, because *Grease 2* was considered both a critical and commercial failure, she had difficulty finding roles despite her individually excellent performance in it.

   For example, Michelle was only able to get cast in roles that portrayed her as a "bimbo" or "sexpot" after *Grease 2*, and it wasn't until 5 years later that she would have another chance in a big role that would allow her to show her true talent (1983's *Scarface*). And after this, her talent brought her a type of worldwide fame that became overwhelming.

   Even though Michelle dreamt about what it would be like to be famous, being famous was a different experience altogether. She realized that she couldn't go shopping or out like a normal person, for example, and she realized that her every move would be watched (and photographed) by the paparazzi. For her—and for nearly every icon who has ever discussed fame—this was a difficult adjustment that never became easy to accept (even after many years in the limelight).

   The lesson here is that we might think we want something (i.e., fame like Michelle), but when we get it, we may be more overwhelmed with the downsides of the thing we originally wanted than the upsides of it. So, we have to not only be careful what we wish for, but we also have to prepare for what we wish for—both the good parts of it, as well as the bad parts.

> "I don't know if it's naivete or narcissism, but I start out with this notion that I can do anything. It's not until I get into it that I realize what I've thrown myself into, and then I will do anything not to humiliate myself. And that, I think, is the secret to my success."

2. Success begins when you start, not when you achieve.

Michelle has suffered from imposter's syndrome—the idea that you are going to be exposed as a fraud—because she never had formal training in acting. She thought she would just "learn as she goes."

But her imposter syndrome was made worse by the fact that she was considered "the hot girl," which made her very insecure because she didn't know if she was getting roles for her talent or her looks. Nevertheless, it was partly her insecurity that drove her to work so hard at her craft so that she could become enormously successful in it. After all, she didn't want to embarrass herself in something everyone thought she could do (including herself).

The takeaway is that, even if we experience insecurity, imposter's syndrome, or other self-esteem issues, we should still dive in head first to reach for our dreams. Sure, we might be scared while we do it, but it will just mean that we will have to put in the extra effort like Michelle to make sure we become excellent at what we do (even if we don't initially know what we're doing).

> "The anticipation of something is always much worse than the reality."

3. The worst part about fear is thinking about it, not living through it.

As an actress constantly being judged for her looks, Michelle would often second guess herself going to auditions and onto set. And as a consequence, she always feared the worst even if it never happened.

But even if the worst did happen, she would realize that the horrible nightmare she had worked up in her head was 10x more hellish than experiencing the reality of the thing. Even being blacklisted for her role in Grease 2, for example, was not as difficult as she thought it would be—it was actually just the beginning of what would become an iconic career.

For you and me, we can learn that often the worst part of fear is thinking about it, not living through it. But even if a few of our fears do happen to come true, we can learn from Michelle that the reality of them is often nowhere near as bad as what we thought they would be.

> **"Love humiliates you."**

4. When you truly love something—or someone—you must fully surrender your ego to it.

After starting the Via Rosa production company, Michelle ran it for 10 years with the idea that it would help her secure strong female roles. And it did.

For example, she was able to play Catwoman in *Batman Returns* as well as a life-changing teacher role in *Dangerous Minds*. And she did this because these were the roles she always wanted to play.

But then something happened. Michelle shut down Via Rosa because she loved something even more than these parts: her family. She decided to semi-retire so that she could raise her kids in a somewhat normal environment which seemed crazy to the world (i.e., why would you give up such a great career?) but that was perfectly sensible to her.

The lesson here is that surrendering to what you love most will sometimes humiliate you in the eyes of others. It will humiliate you because some people won't understand your choices and decisions (i.e., walking away from fame and fortune for family), but ultimately that is what true love does. And the more loving a person you become, the more this lesson will sink it.

> "The less you focus on your flaws, the better off you are."

5. Never meditate on what makes you weak, meditate on what makes you strong.

As Michelle reached her 40s and 50s, she became more and more confident. For example, she felt like she didn't have to be the hot girl anymore and could instead focus on being a great actress.

Because of this transition, it allowed her to take her eyes off of her looks and put them completely on her roles. Of course, she had always done this, but she was especially able to do this in her 40s and 50s because she felt more secure in who she was compared to when she was in her 20s and 30s.

For you and me, we can learn that the less we focus on our flaws, the more confident we will become. For it is only when we learn to appreciate ourselves—and truly meditate on who we are, not criticize who we are not—that we will start oozing with the kind of happiness and charisma that we need to live our best lives. Just like Michelle.

SUMMARY: LIFE LESSONS FROM MICHELLE PFEIFFER

- What you dream of is often very different from what you actually experience.
- Making the decision to start is a vital component of success.

- A fearful thought is often worse than experiencing the reality of that fear.
- Surrender your ego to the person or thing you love.
- Meditate on your strengths to magnify them even bigger.

"Dream as if you'll live forever. Live as if you'll die today."

—James Dean

CHAPTER 26

JAMES DEAN

James Dean was an American actor who shot to fame in the 1950s. He starred in films ranging from *Rebel Without A Cause*, *East of Eden*, and *Icon*. And he became the only actor to be nominated for two posthumous Academy Awards.

But growing up, life was hard for him. James's mother died when he was just 9 years old, for example, and he had to work odd jobs like being a parking lot attendant before he got his big break in films. But even when he did get his break, it was short lived: his life was cut tragically short at just 25 years of age when he died in a car accident in northern California. Nevertheless, James's legend grew in his death and he is considered one of the greatest icons of all time.

> "Only the gentle are ever really strong."

1. The strongest people in the world are the most loving.

When James was growing up, he experienced much hardship. His father, for example, abandoned his family and his mother died when he was just a boy.

However, James was also sexually molested as a youngster. But instead of letting these traumatic incidents define him—or hold him back—he pushed ahead toward his dream and committed to treating everyone he met with kindness and respect. Even though he had every reason to be bitter, he chose to be gentle in his short life.

The takeaway from this is that hardship can either break us or make us the most resilient and compassionate individuals in the world. But it is up to us to choose who we want to be (either bitter people or better people).

> "The gratification comes in the doing, not in the results."

2. True meaning and success is found in the pursuit of your dream, not just the attainment of it.

Unlike other icons and legends, James did not have the opportunity to act in many films. But the films he did act in were extraordinary.

For example, James was able to cement his legacy in Hollywood forever for his performance in *Rebel Without A Cause*. Interestingly enough, though, his goal in the film was to learn and grow as an artist—not just deliver an award-winning performance. For James, satisfaction was found in the doing, in the journey, and not in simply the attainment of the end result.

What we can learn from this is that the more we focus on the process of reaching a goal or a dream, the happier we will become in our day to day lives and the more we will appreciate all that we experience. So, when we slow down to enjoy what we're doing—and not just focus on where we're going—we will multiply our immediate joy.

> "Am I in love? Absolutely. I'm in love with ancient philosophers, foreign painters, classic authors, and musicians who have died long ago."

3. Look to the greatest figures of the past to accelerate your progress in the present.

For such a young person, James had a very old soul. And part of the reason this may have been is because of all of the life he had lived in his very short 25 years.

For example, in addition to acting, he also took an avid interest in bullfighting, car racing, and pillow talk. Yes, pillow talk. James had an active love life and was remembered by his girlfriends as having very deep intellectual and emotional conversations about everything under the sun because he was interested in the history and possibilities of many things.

For you and me, we can recognize that the broader our knowledge, the more interesting conversationalists we will become. But we can also recognize that the broader our knowledge, the more passionate people we can become by putting ourselves in positions to develop an intense relationship with the best people—and things—that came before us by studying them deeply.

> "I think the prime reason for existence, for living in this world is discovery."

4. If there was nothing new to see or experience in life, what is the point?

James loved to race his sports cars. In fact, he competed actively in races and his dream was to one day compete in the Indianapolis 500 (though some of his movie studios banned him from racing while he was actively shooting a film for them).

Nevertheless, James was still able to race in Palm Springs, Bakersfield, and Santa Barbara. And part of the reason he raced is because he wanted to experience the world in a different way—

and at a different level—than he ever had before. Unfortunately, he took this too far (his racing led to his untimely death, but in life it gave him the great thrills he was looking for.)

What we can take away from this is that we should be open to exploring new things and developing our interests. Of course, we should never put ourselves in harm's way, but we should make an effort to try to experience as much of this life as possible so that we will know what it is like to be fully alive.

> "Remember: life is short, break the rules."

5. You have no time to fit in the square box others are trying to force you into.

The heroic part about James's life is that he took risks on behalf of himself—and on behalf of his dreams. For example, he moved to Los Angeles, enrolled at UCLA, but dropped out after only a semester so that he could pursue acting full time. Although this seems more common today, dropping out of school then was frowned upon, but to James he felt it was his shot to make it in the big leagues.

The takeaway is that we can do things that people frown upon if we feel it will help advance our dreams and our goals. Just because they don't understand it—or just because they wouldn't do it themselves—doesn't mean that we should let that stop us. We only have one life and we should live it the way we want to.

SUMMARY: LIFE LESSONS FROM JAMES DEAN

- The most loving people and the strongest people are one and the same.
- The pursuit of your dream – and not just the attainment of your dream – is where true meaning and success is located.
- Accelerate your present progress: study the greatest figures of the past.
- The point of life is to experience new sights and adventures.
- Don't allow people to force you into a square box.

PART II
COMEDIANS

Now, let's change gears a bit and turn our attention to the iconic funny men and women who have defied the odds and made America laugh—and become legends in the process.

Perhaps one of the most interesting things about these breakthrough comedians is just how much they can teach us—and not just lessons about jokes. These comedians have, despite their good cheer and innate humor, had to overcome roadblocks and obstacles that threatened their dreams, made them question themselves, and caused them to almost throw in the towel. And the hard-won wisdom they have learned can help us understand the complexities of the inevitable twists and turns of our own journeys.

Through it all, Hollywood's most iconic funny people have taught us that we can still laugh whether everything is going right in our lives or nothing is. They have taught us that it is okay to laugh at ourselves. And they have taught us that enjoying little lighthearted moments are a big part of what life is about.

Let's jump into the mindset of these legends and see what they have to say.

"You only get one life. I'm going to embrace mine."

—Kevin Hart

CHAPTER 27

KEVIN HART

Kevin Hart is a prolific actor, comedian, and producer. He is considered one of the funniest people in Hollywood, and has appeared in films like *Think Like a Man*, *Ride Along*, *Jumanji*, and *The Secret Life of Pets*, among others.

Growing up in Philadelphia, he was the son of a crack addict who was in and out of jail as well as the son of a single mom. He moved to Boston to become a shoe salesman before eventually finding his way to the standup comedy circuit, which helped get him the recognition he needed to make his way to Hollywood and one day become a legend.

> "Everybody that is successful lays a blueprint out."

1. You must write out the vision you have for your life and how you will get it.

One of Kevin's biggest secrets to success is simply having a plan of action. Like other icons and legends, he doesn't wish or hope for things to happen—he writes them first and then commits to massive action to make them happen.

For example, Kevin launched his own production company—Hartbeat Productions—because he didn't want to just wait for roles or projects to come to him; he wanted to develop things himself so that he could advance himself more quickly than just letting "life happen" to him as so many people do.

The takeaway here is that developing a written plan for your goals is so much more important than most realize. In fact, over 97% of people never write out their goals or vision, so putting the blueprint together for yourself will get you much further than those who don't. And once you have a blueprint in place, it doesn't mean you have to religiously follow it; it just means that you have a GPS that will help keep you on the right track even if you occasionally get caught in a detour.

> "The day you stop doing the small things is the day you think you're above everybody else."

2. The small things are always more important than people realize.

Few people realize that Kevin's company has a deal with Nickelodeon to make content and shows for kids. But the reason Kevin has this deal is because he believes in investing in the next generation, not as an afterthought, but as a priority.

Kevin even takes this philosophy when choosing projects he himself doesn't create. For example, he decided to star in *The Secret Life of Pets*—an animated movie aimed squarely at kids—because he wanted to do a fun project and give kids a chance to hear somebody that sounded like him, which would give them a more inclusive worldview (since African American men have not traditionally voiced lead roles in animated movies).

What we can learn from this is that even a top movie star like Kevin believes that the small things—or in this case, the small ones (kids)—are really what (or who) matter in the long run. For you and me, when we start to see that we are truly role models for those coming after us, it'll become a priority to help show them the way (instead of just focusing on finding our own way).

> "I don't care how busy I am, I will always make time for what is most important to me."

3. Continuously prioritizing what is important is one of the most difficult things you will ever do.

Finding time for what matters is something Kevin loves to do. And an example of this is his love for sports.

For example, even though Kevin is only 5'4, he loves basketball. In fact, he loves it so much that you can see him at many Lakers basketball games courtside with his wife. Even though he is busy and one of the most prolific stars working, he still makes time to regularly watch one of his hobbies in person because it is important to him.

The lesson here is that whether it is a hobby, family, relationship, or something else, we can always make time for what's important to us. Even if you don't currently have the flexibility or power to always prioritize big things like Kevin, you can still prioritize what you do have control over.

> "Whatever you've done, good or bad, it's nothing but preparation for the big events to come."

4. Your entire life is a test.

When Kevin was very young, he initially moved to New York City and then to Boston to be a shoe salesman. But it was during his time as a shoe salesman that he discovered the underground stand-up comedy circuit and fell in love.

But falling in love isn't always easy. For example, Kevin was regularly booed off stage in his early comedic performances and he never felt quite comfortable using his own voice. Nevertheless, he used this humiliation to reflect on how—and what—he should improve so that he would be embraced on stage, not rejected. And once he did, he found himself—and he found his voice—and realized that his early rejection was only setting him up to grow into his authentic self which he would need to become a massive success.

For us, we can realize that all of the moments we've experienced in life—the triumphs and the failures, the successes and the heartbreaks—are really just leading us up to something even bigger and better if only we will learn the right lessons from these things (and if only we will keep the right attitudes about them too).

> "You can do the same thing with $20 million that you can do with $50 million. So, at a certain point in your life and in your career, you realize it's not about money."

5. One day you will realize that enough is truly enough.

Kevin has a net worth north of $200 million dollars. And he earned every bit of it through his relentless work ethic.

However, as Kevin was scoring million dollar paydays, he realized something: that accumulating more and more is not really the purpose of success (or of life). Sure, money can do some things, but the simple accumulation of it holds no inherent value itself. And, as Kevin noted, after a certain point (i.e., when you have all of the homes, cars, clothes, and toys you want), it doesn't add much to your life.

The takeaway here is that one day we will realize how much is truly enough for us. One day we will see that our money is neither good nor bad, but simply a tool for negotiating our way through life—for the things we want and for the things we don't. And as soon as that day comes for us, we will reach a much healthier place in our lives.

SUMMARY: LIFE LESSONS FROM KEVIN HART

- Write out the adventure map of your life and start exploring it.
- The most important things in life are often the overlooked ones.
- Continuously prioritize what is important in your life.
- Your entire life is a test, not just certain moments.
- Decide that enough is truly enough.

"If you work really hard, and you're kind, amazing things will happen."

—Conan O'Brien

CHAPTER 28

CONAN O'BRIEN

Conan O'Brien is one of the funniest people ever to grace Hollywood. After starting as a writer on *Saturday Night* Live and *The Simpsons*, he transitioned into late-night television where he has been a star for decades—and which enabled him to be named as one of the 100 Most Influential People in the World by *Time Magazine*.

Conan dedicated his life to comedy early, having been editor of *The Harvard Lampoon* and a comedian before getting his big break. But he hasn't just stuck to entertaining people or making them laugh. He has also started anti-hunger organizations and opened up meal centers to feed those who are on the brink of dying due to starvation.

CONAN O'BRIEN'S TOP 5 LIFE LESSONS

> "Is it possible for a grown man to be body shamed by his own mirror?"

1. Humility is one the most overlooked qualities in success.

What makes Conan different from so many other comedians is how humble and self-deprecating he is. For example, Conan often pokes fun at himself instead of his guests. He once even had fellow comedian Will Ferrell partially shave his beard on live television just for laughs at his own expense.

But time and time again, Conan has shown his humility over the years by refusing to hurt others with his comedy and instead take the punch himself. His podcast entitled "Conan O'Brien Needs A Friend" is the epitome of how he has used self-deprecating humor to advance in Hollywood - and in life.

For you and me, the lesson we can learn from Conan is that you can be both humble and successful at the same time. You don't need to hurt others, and you don't need to be anybody other than yourself to make it at whatever you feel called to do.

> "Every generation just wants their kids to have a better Spiderman reboot than they did."

2. Building a better future for the next generation is critically important.

Few people know that Conan O'Brien has made significant sacrifices in his career to create a stable and protective environment for his children. For example, he had an opportunity to move back to New York (the home of late night television) from Los Angeles to advance professionally, but refused because he did not want to subject his kids to a move that would disrupt their lives.

But in addition to not disrupting his own kids' lives so they could feel loved and supported, he has also felt it very important that the kind of comedy he creates doesn't disrupt other people's lives too. That is, Conan believes in being a role model and does not want to subject young kids to ruthless or nasty comedy that could damage their sense of self over the long run. As a result, his comedy tends to be more PG-13 than R or rated X.

The lesson that can be learned is that creating a world that will allow upcoming generations to prosper is the greatest legacy that can be left behind. In practical terms this means that in our personal and professional lives, we should always be thinking about how to strengthen young people so they can grow up stronger and wiser than we did.

> "All I ask is one thing, and I'm asking particularly of young people: please don't be cynical. I hate cynicism, for the record, it's my least favorite quality and it doesn't lead anywhere."

3. Dreams are not buried in failure, they're buried in doubt.

Because people, especially young people, have been hurt, it is easy for them to become cynical, disillusioned, and skeptical towards life. But Conan believes that when you buy into cynicism your soul dies a long, painful death.

In Conan's life, even though things seem perfect he himself has had moments where things were not going well for him. For example, not only was he humiliated after being terminated from *The Tonight Show* (through no fault of his own), but he has also been falsely accused and sued over "joke stealing." But despite this, he has decided to remain optimistic because otherwise the weight of doubt—not to mention the weight of adversity and opposition from others—is enough to sink one's career (and life).

For you and me, the wisdom we can glean is that remaining hopeful and optimistic about our futures is the only way we can have any kind of long-term happiness and success.

> "There are few things in this life more liberating than having your worst fear realized."

4. Overcoming your nightmares make you unstoppable.

Being famous is not all it's cracked up to be. For example, although Conan has a squeaky clean image, he still deals with stalkers, bullies, and dangerous wackos—one of the downsides of being an icon in today's age.

In one particularly egregious incident, Conan dealt with a stalker who was making death threats against him for not inviting him on his show. Even though this stalker was told to stay away from Conan, this stalker tried to force his way into the studio to go after Conan.

Surviving this situation—and others—showed Conan that even when dreams turn into nightmares you can become unstoppable once you beat those nightmares back into submission.

> "Remember that the story is never over."

5. You will never stop being a work-in-progress.

Many people want to retire if they reach a certain level of success or want to quit if they've hit a roadblock. But not Conan. Even though he knows he could retire with his $150 million dollar fortune, he chooses not to because he still feels he has not hit his peak level of creativity or performance.

What we can learn from this is that no matter who we are or how old we get, we can always become better if we choose to. We will be works in progress until the day we leave the earth.

SUMMARY: LIFE LESSONS FROM CONAN O'BRIEN

- One of the most overlooked attributes of success is humility.
- It's critically important to build the platform on which the next generation can stand.
- Doubt, not failure, buries dreams.
- Be unstoppable by battling through your nightmares.
- You are always a work in progress.

"I always knew I shouldn't have said that."

—Jon Stewart

CHAPTER 29
JON STEWART

Jon Stewart is a 22 x Emmy winning comedian, talk show host, and satirist who brought humor to politics and cable television in a way never seen before. Not only did he write, produce, and host his iconic *The Daily Show* for 16 seasons, but he helped create *The Colbert Report* and launch the careers of numerous other successful comedians including Stephen Colbert, Steve Carrel, and John Oliver.

But prior to his breakout success, Jon was a puppeteer for children with disabilities, a soccer coach for kids, and a bartender, which he credits with helping to spark his creativity and drive to be on television. He is a staunch advocate for 9/11 first responders and has opened up sanctuary farms for abused animals, among many other great things he has done in life.

JON STEWART'S TOP 5 LIFE LESSONS

> "If you don't stick to your values when they're being tested, they're not values: they're hobbies."

1. Icons hold onto their beliefs even when they're not convenient.

   Jon has been described as an equal opportunity satirist, meaning he will call out politicians on both sides of the aisle if they are acting hypocritical or doing something wrong. And although he sometimes got in trouble for this, he decided he had to use his platform to spread truth, not political party talking points or propaganda.

   For example, Jon famously went on one of CNN's top rated political debate shows, *Crossfire*, and told the Republican and Democratic co-hosts that instead of educating America, they were simply adding unnecessary noise. And in true fashion, the co-hosts attacked Jon, but he was unwilling to back down from their criticism. (Ironically, CNN executives eventually canceled *Crossfire* because they believed that Jon was right and their own anchors were wrong.)

   The lesson we can learn from Jon is that we should always be willing to stick to our beliefs even if it means being criticized from others who we are holding accountable because we can truly change things if we are unwilling to back down. In other words, we do not need to hide or run away from our values (i.e., speaking the truth) as it can help change people's minds to behave in more appropriate ways.

> "If we amplify everything, we hear nothing."

2. Become quiet enough to recognize the difference between the important and the trivial.

Jon began hosting *The Daily Show* around the time that cable news became a 24 hour, 7 days a week phenomenon that would re-play the most controversial news stories of the day over and over again. And it was in this context he realized that newsmakers weren't interested in solving America's problems but instead gossiping about them—and making money from them.

But to Jon, he thought this wasn't improving the state of the country, so he wanted to use his own satirical show to poke fun at how trivial most of this behavior (and business strategy) was from 24 hour cable news. For example, Jon would call out on-air news personalities (from the left and the right) for distorting the facts of a story to sensationalize it, fit a narrative, or to increase the ratings. Of course, the on-air personalities responded negatively, but Jon believed it was his responsibility to highlight what was truly important from what was being over-hyped by the personalities and cable news outlets to fit a corporate agenda of profiteering.

The takeaway here is that we must learn to get to a quiet enough (or reflective enough) place in our life and work to understand the difference between the meaningful and the trivial because society won't do this for us. In other words, we have to discern the difference between what matters and what doesn't because what the news tells us matters usually doesn't—in the long run.

> "I have complete faith in the continued absurdity of whatever's going on."

3. Learn to develop a sense of perspective about the wackiness of life.

Everyone has a little bit of a hypocrite in them, and Jon knows this. However, it is when he would see politicians who would blatantly flip flop on consequential issues that would really stir his ire on people's outright absurdities.

Jon would see very powerful and important presidential candidates or political leaders, for example, who would look at the polls and change their long-held views on issues just to get an endorsement or financial contribution, a few more votes, or look better in a news story. And this sickened him. So, as a consequence, he learned to recognize that much of what goes on in politics—and life—can be completely wacky and not make much logical sense because people are simply operating out of short-sighted self-interest much of the time.

For you and me, if we understand that life and society can be absurd, we will learn to be less shocked at how outrageous other people sometimes act.

> "I'm not going to censor myself to comfort your ignorance."

4. You possess information others do not, so do not be afraid to educate them about it.

Although many people think it is easier to be outspoken if you're rich and famous like Jon, they often don't consider that it might be harder than they realize. For example, when Jon discusses controversial issues, not only does he risk offending people, but he risks losing financial sponsors, getting bullied on social media, and facing potential backlash.

For example, Jon called out a prominent news organization for misrepresenting facts around the police shooting of an unarmed Black man which caused an instant firestorm (and for Jon to lose some fans and support). For many people, it would have been easier to avoid not commenting on such a hot button political issue, but Jon wanted to make sure to inform and empower people who may not otherwise question their news sources (who, in this case, was deliberating distorting facts to fit their audiences' political persuasions).

The takeaway here: even if we might get some pushback, we should nevertheless not be afraid to speak our truth especially if we believe others do not possess the same information we have—or if they are trying to exploit the information we have (or particular stories) to fit their own agendas.

> "The more you delve into science, the more it appears to rely on faith."

5. The greatest minds realize they don't know much of anything.

Jon is a committed liberal and generally backs democratic causes, but that does not mean he sticks to the party line. For example, he has voted for Republicans and he regularly called out politicians from his side of the aisle if they made a faux paus. And part of the reason he did this is because he realized early on that not only does he not possess a monopoly on truth, but that he doesn't possess a monopoly on facts either.

In our own lives, when we come to see that no matter how smart, how logical, how evidence- based, or how scientific the things—or the people—we believe in are, much of what has been learned (or believed) up until now is still speculation and faith (not hard facts). That is, we only know a tiny fraction of knowledge and will only ever know a tiny fraction of knowledge even if we get 20 PhDs. Recognizing this reality should help to give us humility and perspective—and just a little more grace toward others who do not agree with us because they might know a bit more than we do (or put less emphasis on the same facts that we exalt).

SUMMARY: LIFE LESSONS FROM JON STEWART

- Hold onto your beliefs even when they're inconvenient.
- Recognize the difference between what is perceived as trivial and important.
- Know that with life comes a lot of absurdities.
- Educate people on the knowledge they do not possess.
- Even great minds realize they possess little knowledge in the grand scale of the universe.

"I'm not funny. What I am is brave."

—Lucille Ball

CHAPTER 30

LUCY BALL

Lucille Ball—known simply as Lucy—was a 4x Emmy winner, first female owner of a major Hollywood production company and studio, and star of the number #1 show in America, *I Love Lucy*. She was the recipient of the Presidential Medal of Freedom, inducted into the Television Hall of Fame, and is considered by many to be the most legendary female entertainer in history.

But Lucy came from humble beginnings. She moved around a lot as a child, for example, was forbidden by her grandparents to look at herself in the mirror while growing up, and was even told by her acting teacher she would never be successful in Hollywood because she was untalented.

Nevertheless, Lucy became iconic and learned many lessons on her unbelievable journey that we can take with us on ours.

LUCY BALL'S TOP LIFE LESSONS

> "Love yourself first and everything else falls into line. You really have to love yourself to get anything done in this world."

1. The world doesn't need to accept you, you need to accept you.

   Lucy was told she wasn't talented enough to be successful and was never really given a big breakout role early in her career. For example, she was rejected from a part in *Gone with the Wind* and was known as "Queen of the Bs'"—that is, she was known as an actress who could only appear in mediocre films.

   However, Lucy did not let this early disappointment deter her from showing her talent to the world. She persisted on and, even though CBS was not impressed with the pilot episode of her dream show *I Love Lucy*, they eventually aired it. And, as they say, the rest is history.

   The lesson here is that regardless of the obstacles and opposition that come your way, you must believe so strongly in yourself that nothing can stop you from getting where you are meant to be. Your destiny will never automatically happen, you must fight for it—and you fight for it by believing in and loving yourself.

> "I think knowing what you cannot do is more important than knowing what you can."

2. Building your life on your strengths and not your weaknesses will multiply your success.

As strange as it sounds, Lucy did not believe that she was funny. But what she did believe is that she could tell funny stories about her life that other people could relate to. And this critical recognition—that she was not a comedian, but instead somebody who could act in funny situations—made all of the difference.

For example, Lucy had not only one hit show in her life (*I Love Lucy*), but several. She also starred in the long running series *The Lucy Show* and *Here's Lucy* and used the same formula to be successful in both: poking fun at herself through stories audiences could relate to rather than telling jokes (like comedians).

What we can learn from this is that if we understand what we are good at—and what we're not— and double down on it, we can find massive success without having to reinvent the wheel. Lucy used a formula to win that, by the way, another show (i.e., Seinfeld) followed decades later to great success. All we have to do is find what we're not good at—and then what we're good at—and follow what works.

> "Don't let the brightness of the big goal blind you to what happens on the way toward the goal."

3. Happiness is found in the journey, not the destination.

Even though Lucy became a massive success and achieved iconic goals, the reason she performed was because she found such joy doing it. For example, Lucy only wanted to perform in front of live studio audiences whether they be for her television shows or for her comedic tours because hearing laughter from people spoke to her soul in a way that money, fame, and awards never could. Lucy needed the energy and excitement of hearing how she was touching other people's lives in real-time more than anything else.

In our own lives, we should pursue work that allows us to enjoy the day-to-day as well and not just the shiny rewards at the end. If we do, life will be dramatically different than if we are chasing only after trophies that can never fill our hearts.

> "One of the things I learned the hard way was that it doesn't pay to get discouraged. Keeping busy and making optimism a way of life can restore faith in yourself."

4. Assassinate all discouragement in your life if you want to achieve great things.

Lucy could have easily gotten discouraged given all of the setbacks and failures she faced. Despite being a ratings juggernaut early in her career, for example, when she starred in the show *Life with Lucy*, it was such a critical and commercial failure that the show was canceled after only 3 months.

But Lucy also faced other failures too, particularly in her personal life. She divorced her husband and business partner Desi Arnaz after telling a California court that life with him was a "nightmare" despite the fake image the *I Love Lucy Show* portrayed their relationship as. And even though this was healthy for Lucy to do, financially it cost her as she had to buy out Desi from the studio they jointly owned and run it by herself.

Nevertheless, Lucy never let the ups and downs of her personal or professional life stop her from staying optimistic about the future. The lesson for you and me should be the same: even if we have been discouraged or disappointed by something in the past, we should put in the tough mental and emotional work to overcome it so that we can be positive about ourselves and work toward building better lives.

> "Not everything that is faced can be changed, but nothing can be changed until it is faced."

5. Running toward your problems—not away from them—is the only way you can get the victory you deserve.

As a young person, Lucy registered as a member of the communist party to appease her socialist grandfather. However, the "communist" label did not escape her and, in fact, caused her to land in some hot water during the height of U.S.-Soviet Union tensions.

For example, the FBI started to keep files on Lucy's political activities which caused the House Un-American Activities Committee to call Lucy to testify under significant pressure. But instead of running from this witch hunt, Lucy agreed and honestly answered all questions about her past activities instead of pleading the 5th (and not talking).

The lesson that can be learned from this is that when we are courageous like Lucy, we can face our problems so that we can move past them and not hide or take the easy way out by avoiding them.

SUMMARY: LIFE LESSONS FROM LUCY BALL

- After you're done rejecting yourself, start accepting yourself.
- You can multiply your success by developing your strengths, not your weaknesses.
- Finding happiness in the journey is the goal.
- When you achieve great things you often kill off discouragement.
- You grab victory by running toward your problems.

"To be able to truly laugh you must be able to take your pain and play with it!"

—Charlie Chapman

CHAPTER 31

CHARLIE CHAPLIN

Charlie Chaplin was one of the great actors of the silent film era, and one of the funniest actors of all time. Starring in films ranging from The Circus to The Great Dictator, Charlie became an international phenomenon who wrote, directed, acted in, and distributed his own films in Hollywood to great success.

But growing up life was rough for Charlie. His father died when he was young, his mother was committed to a mental institution, and he was even referred to the National Society for the Prevention of Cruelty to Children in Great Britain given his impoverished circumstances.

Nevertheless, Charlie started performing in theatre as a teenager to make ends meet and eventually found his way to Tinseltown vis-a-vis vaudeville. He went on to develop the world famous "Tramp" character which he performed in over 25 films, and is considered by many to be the greatest rags-to-riches story ever in Hollywood.

CHARLIE CHAPMAN'S TOP LIFE LESSONS:

> "Our knowledge has made us cynical. Our cleverness, hard and unkind. We think too much and feel too little. More than machinery we need humanity. More than cleverness we need kindness and gentleness. Without these qualities, life will be violent and all will be lost..."

1. A head full of knowledge must always be matched by a heart full of love.

Charlie dropped out of school to start performing in a traveling group at the age of 13 but one of the things he unfortunately encountered throughout his worldwide travels was brilliant people who were working toward destructive ends. For example, Charlie's life was deeply impacted by both World War 1 and World War 2, and he could not understand how intelligent people like Adolf Hitler could be so evil in mistreating and hurting millions of people.

But Charlie could also not understand how other smart people—like medical doctors, lawyers, and the like—could blindly follow somebody like Hitler and follow his orders given all of their intelligence and "supposed" training. To Charlie, he realized that knowledge alone will not stop people from being cruel to one another. Instead, he believed that only love could do that.

The lesson we can learn from this is that even though we are not facing circumstances like World War 2 and the Nazis, we should nevertheless understand that the only way we can coexist with others on the planet is by loving them. Being offended or trying to cancel others because it "makes sense" to us does not move humanity forward, so we should attempt to heal and understand by growing the love we have in our hearts toward other people.

> "That's the trouble with the world. We all despise ourselves."

2. Self-hatred is more common than self-love.

Charlie grew up seeing hate and war first hand. In fact, he developed one of his most famous movies, *The Dictator*, in response to what he believed was the self-hatred and destruction perpetrated by Adolf Hitler.

But Charlie saw that self-hatred was one of the biggest problems facing other people too. To counter this, he developed the self-deprecating "Tramp" figure to not only give people laughs, but to show them they didn't have to take themselves so seriously even in the age of nuclear weapons.

For you and me, our takeaway is that endlessly criticizing ourselves will not make ourselves better - nor will it make the world better. Instead, we should learn to be more light hearted and see ourselves in a more compassionate way by practicing proven self-love techniques.

> "Life can be wonderful if you're not afraid of it."

3. Victory goes to the bold, not the cautious.

Even though Charlie escaped poverty, rose to global fame, and became the highest paid actor in the world, his life wasn't always easy. For example, the FBI launched a smear campaign against Charlie because they believed he might have been a communist (he was not). But as a result, Charlie somehow ended up on trial, which became one of the biggest scandals in media and legal history (for which he was acquitted).

Nevertheless, Charlie continued to create and act—and he continued to boldly discuss his political beliefs (he referred to himself as a "peacemonger"). This eventually led him to being banned by the United States (his permit was revoked as he was originally from the UK), but he still stayed true to himself—and still kept smiling in the process—and found success in film from overseas.

What we can learn from this is that boldness is our friend and can lead us to the greatness that is within us if we don't shy away from it. However, we can also learn that this boldness can sometimes lead us in hot water (i.e., Charlie's outspoken political beliefs did this to him) but can simultaneously help guide us out of it too.

> "Nothing is permanent in this wicked world—not even our troubles."

4. The only thing that will never change is that things will always change.

As mentioned, Charlie encountered much difficulty in his childhood and throughout his life. From poverty to political accusations to paternity battles, Charlie faced a barrage of negative events that could have left the best of us broken.

But what Charlie realized as well is that even after he faced these things, life would always present another opportunity. A second chance. A do-over. And the ability to make beauty from ashes. For example, after Charlie was kicked out of the United States, he was able to relocate to Switzerland so that he could make the kinds of films he wanted to make—and express the kind of political beliefs he wanted to express.

The takeaway from this is that no matter how bad life seems, things will change if you can outlast the difficult moments just one day at a time.

> "You'll never find a rainbow if you're looking down."

5. To elevate to the higher you cannot stay focused on the lower.

All Charlie ever wanted to do was make people laugh. And he did this at a time—during World Wars 1 and 2—when laughter was needed the most.

What Charlie concluded was that, even in the face of hundreds of millions of deaths the world experienced during his lifetime, you have to stay optimistic in order to even make it through the night sometimes.

In our own lives, if we stay focused on what's ahead—and what's above—we can overcome almost anything that is thrown our way.

SUMMARY: LIFE LESSONS FROM CHARLIE CHAPMAN

- Combine a head full of knowledge with a heart full of love.
- Self-love is much rarer than self-hate these days.
- Boldness, not caution, captures victory.
- Things will always change in your life even if you don't want them to.
- Focusing on the lower level will thwart your ability to capture the higher one.

"A tree falls the way it leans. Be careful the way you lean."

—Danny DeVito

CHAPTER 32

DANNY DEVITO

Danny DeVito is a Golden Globe and Emmy Award winning actor and producer. He is best known for his roles in *Batman Returns*, *Twins*, and *It's Always Sunny in Philadelphia*, among other great projects.

But his rise to fame and fortune was not a typical one. He was diagnosed with Fairbanks Disease growing up—leaving him standing only 4 feet 10 inches tall—and became a professional makeup artist before he eventually found his way to Hollywood. But it was his tenacity and sense of humor that forced Hollywood to pay attention to him—and which eventually made him a legend.

> "The whole point of love is to put someone else's needs above your own."

1. **True love abandons selfishness.**

   Danny loves what he does. But he doesn't just love acting. He also loves producing too, which has caused him to put others before himself given the nature of the role.

   For example, Danny was the producer of *Pulp Fiction*, *Reno 911*, and *Erin Brocovich*, and as producer he was responsible for making sure everyone's needs were met even before his. As a producer, Danny had to make his artistic and financial interests secondary to others on the productions just so that he could pull them together and make them work. This required an incredible amount of humility, selflessness, and looking out for other people that only love made possible.

   The takeaway here is that if you love something—or someone—you will put them before yourself. Now this doesn't mean letting them take advantage of you or sacrificing your self-care, but it does mean that you should look out for #2 or #3 before you look out for #1—especially if you have the ability (or responsibility) to.

> "You have to give people permission to laugh."

2. Always give people the room to be themselves.

Although Danny has appeared in a mixture of dramatic and comedic roles, he really loves making people laugh. And laughter, he believes, is his best gift because it lightens people up.

In the movie *Twins*, for example, he starred opposite the massively-sized Arnold Schwarzenegger as Arnold's "miniature" twin separated at birth. In the film, Danny—who did not know Arnold's character initially—played an orphan who seduced a nun to escape from an orphanage so that he could live a life of small-time crime, which led him to be put in jail for unpaid parking tickets.

Because Danny (and Arnold) played the part with such humor and grace—and allowed people to laugh around the world—audiences rewarded his film with a box office that was 2,000 x its production budget. And it was all because Danny wanted to give people permission to laugh through his funny character.

The lesson here is not that you have to become a comedian or star in a funny movie to make people laugh. It is that people will reward you if you let them drop their guard, open up, and see the bright side of life. Whether that is just using your smile, giving somebody a sincere compliment or telling a polite joke at work, when you give people permission to laugh or feel good about themselves, good things usually will happen for you.

> "I think you do your best work when you take chances, when you're not safe, when you're not in the middle of the road."

3. Greatness happens when you become the most extreme version of yourself.

   One of Danny's greatest performances was when he played The Penguin in Tim Burton's *Batman Returns*. And his performance was great because he took a chance on playing a character who had never been portrayed in such a dark and sinister way before.

   For example, prior to Danny's heroic portrayal as one of Batman's nemeses, The Penguin was always a villain, but audiences never felt fear, suspense, or horror by the character. Danny changed that. At just 4'10, he made loyal Batman fans worry that the little penguin man was going to not only destroy Batman but also haunt their dreams. Because Danny decided to boldly and dramatically play The Penguin in an extreme way, he turned it into an iconic performance that helped make the film one of the all-time greats.

   For you and me, we can learn that it is when we learn to make extreme choices—and not just modest ones—that we can start doing our best work. And by extreme choices I mean when we depart from conventional wisdom or the way everybody else is doing something we have a shot at greatness. But it is up to us.

   > "A bad salesman will automatically drop his price. Bad salesmen make me sick."

4. If you have something valuable, don't give it away for nothing.

   Top actors often get paid enormous sums of money not only because they can command an audience, but also because they can attract the top crew to make a film or project work. Danny certainly falls into this category.

As an actor and producer, for example, Danny has been able to amass a fortune nearing $100 million dollars because he has been excellent at his craft and because he negotiates what he believes he is worth. And in his case, it is millions of dollars per film or television show he performs in or produces.

The lesson here is that if you are good at something, you don't have to give yourself away for free. Whether you can make the kind of cash Danny does or not is irrelevant; all that matters is that you begin to negotiate for yourself what you think your product or service is worth. Not only will people respect you, but you will learn to respect you.

> "There are two dilemmas that rattle the human mind: how do you hang onto someone who won't stay? And how do you get rid of someone who won't go?"

5. Curating the right circle will be one of the greatest challenges of your life.

Although separated from his wife of 30 years, Rhea Perlman, Danny still considers her one of his very best friends. But he also considers her as one of his chief artistic confidantes.

For numerous projects, for example, Danny has also acted alongside his Emmy Award winning wife. Whether in *Matilda* or the show *Taxi*, Danny and Rhea have been side by side because they felt that they needed each other to grow personally and professionally.

For us, finding the right people who will support and challenge us to go to the next level will be one of our biggest opportunities—and challenges—in life. But regardless of whether people stay or go, the right people will help us grow at the right times in our lives, so it behooves us to learn who the right people are.

SUMMARY: LIFE LESSONS FROM DANNY DEVITO

- When you abandon selfishness you will discover true love.
- Give people space to be themselves.
- Becoming the most extreme version of yourself allows greatness to happen.
- Don't give away your most valuable assets.
- One of the greatest challenges of life is curating the right social circle.

PART III
DIRECTORS & STUDIO WIZARDS

Icons and legends come in all flavors, and directors and studio creators are no different. In this section, we will learn from the people who have created blockbuster movie studios; launched multibillion dollar franchises; helped define the childhood of millions; challenged the political and economic status quo; and who have reinvented the very definition of what it means to be a Hollywood director.

From Steven Spielberg to George Lucas, Walt Disney to Stan Lee and beyond, these iconic filmmakers had to not only invent themselves and their artistic styles, but they often had to invent new technologies that made their artistic styles and dreams come true.

Although these creators have turned their films into "events" and existential experiences, in many cases it did not come easy for them. And the lessons we can learn from their struggles, from their valleys, and from their pain can serve us well as we embark on doing new and challenging things in our own lives.

Let's step onto their sets and look at the world through their lens to see the specific things they can teach us.

When I grow up, I still want to be a director."

— Steven Spielberg

CHAPTER 33

STEVEN SPIELBERG

Steven Spielberg is arguably the greatest director of all time. He has directed over 100 films including *Jurassic Park, Jaws, Schindler's List, E.T.,* and *Ready Player One,* and has produced even more. Not only have his movies been nominated for 11 Academy Awards, but they've made more than $25 billion dollars at the box office, cementing Steven as a legend for the ages.

But Steven's path to Hollywood was anything but guaranteed. Not only was he turned down from the USC School of Cinematic Arts—considered one of the top film schools in the world—but his early attempts to make it as a director were rejected by Tinseltown with multiple of his projects being turned down or opening to very mixed reviews.

Nevertheless, Steven persisted and was finally able to make his first feature film, The Sugarland Express, which helped him gain the credibility to make his next movie, Jaws, which in turn brought him worldwide acclaim.

STEVEN SPIELBERG'S TOP 5 LIFE LESSONS

> "All of us every single year, we're a different person. I don't think we're the same person all our lives."

1. We have to be willing to become new—and better—versions of ourselves over and over again.

Steven believes that with each new film that he makes, he is a different (and better) person than he was compared to the films he made before. And he doesn't just believe that he is more skilled at his craft, but he believes he is more personally and professionally empathetic, and sees the world in a bigger and more unique way.

For example, Spielberg doesn't think he could have made the movie *E.T.* until he became a father in real life (which helped shape how he thought about the movie). The same is true with other films he made in his career: whether with *Jurassic Park* or *Saving Private Ryan*, how Steven was learning and changing in his real life deeply impacted how he directed his projects. Instead of him just sticking to the approach that worked before—the "if it ain't broke, don't fix it" attitude—Steven deliberately improved himself and his approaches year in and year out to become an even better director (and person).

What you and I can learn from this is that not only is it okay to be different people than we used to be, but that we should strive to be so that we can put a "better us" into all of the work that we do.

> "All of my movies are about how I wish the world would work."

2. Never accept the status quo, improve it.

Steven is sometimes criticized because his movies are considered "wish fulfillment" and often have a "happy ending." But Steven believes that his approaches—seeing things ultimately work out for the best in the end—should be what movies are about. But why?

Steven believes that, given all of the fear and despair in the world, people should be offered hope, fantasy, and positivity when they're watching films not only as an escape, but as a refuge. And he is on to something: his films are consistently considered among the most popular of all time because he knows, deep down, people want to believe in good overcoming evil.

The takeaway from this is that being a bright light in a world of darkness is ultimately what people want—and need—from you. Giving in to being cynical and pessimistic might be fashionable or reasonable, but providing others with hope so that they can improve their lives will be the most important contribution and legacy you can leave behind to your loved ones and humanity.

> "I don't dream at night, I dream at day, I dream all day."

3. It is possible to live your dreams everyday if you simply decide to.

Many people believe that you simply have to be "lucky" like Steven to live your dreams. But the reality is that Steven made decisions to put himself in position to be able to dream all day, every day. And so can you.

Although Steven's early days were difficult—being turned down from film school as well as by numerous investors to make his dream projects—he continued pursuing his passion until "luck" was on his side. In other words, because he refused to say "no" to himself, he continued on until his reality started to match his dreams.

However, this doesn't mean it was always easy for him. For example, his breakout film Jaws was nearly canceled by the studio because it went 100 days over schedule— and wildly over budget. Still, though, Steven was able to make the iconic film he wanted to prove to others that he should be able to dream for a living.

The lesson here is that even if your current reality may not be close to your dreams—and even if many people tell you that you can't live your dreams—you must keep going until you do. Never underestimate your ability to override your current reality with a little bit of persistence.

> "The delicate balance of mentoring someone is not creating them in your own image, but giving them the opportunity to create themselves."

4. The greatest gift you can give to another is helping them become who they are called to be.

Over his 50 year career, Steven has had the opportunity to mentor many up and coming directors, including the directors of *Back to the Future*, *Gremlins*, *Memoirs of a Geisha*, and *Who Framed Roger Rabbit*, among many others. And in each case, Steven did not attempt to force the directors to make the same kinds of creative decisions he would have made if he was the director of these films. Instead, he worked with them to draw out their unique artistic voice so that they could make the movie that was in their heart, not his.

Although Steven contributed deeply to the development of these directors—and their films—he still nevertheless knew when to back off and let these other directors have their say—and the final word, which is no easy feat for somebody as talented and influential as he is.

The takeaway here is that, when grooming the next generation, be sure to let them grow and express themselves so that they become the first version of them, not the second version of you. The more you give people the love, support, and encouragement to develop their own gifts and talents without forcing them into a preconceived box, the more they will surprise you with just how special they truly are.

> "Even though I get older, what I do never gets old, and that's what I think keeps me hungry."

5. Choose a career interesting enough to keep you excited all of your life.

Despite directing over 100 films—and producing more than double that many—Steven has rarely made a sequel in his life. Instead, he has insisted on taking on original projects so that he could continue to challenge himself creatively and intellectually.

For example, after making Jaws, but before making *Raiders of the Lost Ark*, Steven made a comedy film, even though he didn't consider himself a comedic director just to shake things up. He also made a virtual reality film—*Ready Player One*—even though he wasn't an expert at the new technology the film employed (and even though he had never used the new technology before).

What you and I can learn from this is that not only should we continue to challenge ourselves in our work, but we should choose variety in it too so that we can have careers as prolific—and long—as Steven's.

SUMMARY: LIFE LESSONS FROM STEVEN SPIELBERG

- Be willing to become newer and better versions of yourself throughout life.
- Improve a mediocre status quo, don't settle for it.
- Start living your dreams one small decision at a time.
- Help someone else become who they are called to be.
- You will stay excited all of your life if you choose the right career.

"We are all living in cages with the door wide open."

—George Lucas

CHAPTER 34

GEORGE LUCAS

Billionaire filmmaker George Lucas is the creator of two of the most beloved and iconic franchises of all times—*Star Wars* and *Indiana Jones*—along with many other successful endeavors, including Industrial Light and Magic. George also is the first person to attempt to incorporate Pixar's nascent technology into *Star Wars* films—as early as the late 1970s—before selling the company to Steve Jobs (who in turn helped it launch the *Toy Story* franchise).

But growing up, George didn't always want to be a filmmaker. Instead, he wanted to be a professional racecar driver until he was in an accident which caused him to reconsider his career aspirations. After he enrolled at the University of Southern California's School of Cinematic Arts, he cemented his movie-making prowess before moving on to direct Oscar-nominated film *American Graffiti* and others.

GEORGE LUCAS'S TOP 5 LIFE LESSONS

> "You don't always know exactly what you're doing and you shouldn't."

1. Be open to making unexpected detours on your journey to success.

George is a professional experimenter. That is, even with films like *Star Wars*, he is always experimenting with technology, themes, ideas, and more, just so that he can find "what works." Because he doesn't always follow a formula for success, his experiments lead him down unexpected detours that he feels have made him a better creator—and a better storyteller.

For example, after the unexpected success of the first Star Wars film (*Episode IV - A New Hope*), George wanted to try new computer generated imagery for the next film in the franchise so he bought a little known company named Pixar. He poured millions of dollars into it, but it wasn't quite ready to produce the results that it one day did, so George sold it to Steve Jobs. But the lessons that Pixar taught him helped him think about the limits of existing technology—and taught him that he should wait to make later installments of the franchise until technology caught up with his vision.

What you and I can learn from this is that we should always be open to trying new things, especially AFTER we are initially successful. Had George rested on his laurels and relied on the same technology the original Star Wars did, the franchise would not have been the technological (and creative) achievement it became after trying out all sorts of new techniques.

> "If you're really doing something worthwhile, I think you will be pushed to the brink of hopelessness before you come through to the other side."

2. The bigger your goal, the bigger your battle.

Although history looks clear in retrospect, when you're living it, it doesn't always feel that way. And for George, this was certainly the case especially when attempting to realize his vision for Star Wars.

For example, George felt nobody believed in his vision to create a "space opera" (aka Star Wars) so when he made the movie, he refused to shoot it in Los Angeles (an unusual and bold move at the time). Instead, he shot it in northern California so that the studio (Fox) would not give him extra hassle in realizing his vision. But even with this relative autonomy, George still struggled to pull off what he wanted (he will tell you he only achieved 30% of his vision with Star Wars, for example).

The lesson here is there will be external obstacles (other people's opinions or preferences, etc.) and internal ones (not getting everything we want at times, fear, doubt, etc.) when we're attempting to achieve big dreams. And not only do we have to begrudgingly accept this, we must embrace this—just so that our dreams can become somewhat of a reality (and not just stay as the illusion they started out as).

> "Someday you're going to have to separate what seems to be important from what really is important."

3. Greatness lies in recognizing the difference between what is kinda cool from what is absolutely necessary.

One of the most unusual things about George is that after his films were nominated for Academy Awards—and after he had achieved massive success with *Star Wars* and *Indiana Jones*—is that he decided to retire. But he didn't just retire because he was getting older or had the money to retire. He retired for a different reason.

For example, George adopted two children and he decided it was better to raise them being a stay at home (and single) dad than to continue in the prime of his career and influence. For him, raising children who had a father that was always there and loved them tremendously was more important than making the next great movie. (And, for nearly 20 years, he stayed at home before returning to movies once the kids grew up.)

What we can takeaway is that we must truly decide what is important to us—in the short, intermediate, and long-term. And once we decide, we must stick with it even if that means walking away from things that are kinda or really cool just so that we can pursue things that are even more important.

> "My success wasn't based on how I could push down everybody that was around me. My success was based on how much I could push everybody up."

4. There is no higher calling of a leader than to make others better.

George sold *Star Wars* to Disney not because he had to—and not because he needed the money. Rather, George sold *Star Wars* because he wanted there to be a new generation of filmmakers who could bring a fresh take to his beloved creation as he aged and no longer felt he had the capacity to helm the franchise.

This decision—to allow others to live up to their potential and not try to control even his own creation—was based on his belief that you have to believe in others (and not just yourself) as a leader if you want your vision to succeed in the long run.

For you and me, if we start to trust the talent and gifts of others and give them the tools and safety net to develop those things, we can support them as they grow into the best version of themselves. And who wouldn't want to do that to help others?

> "All the skill in the world isn't going to help you unless you have something to say."

5. Take time to develop your unique and original voice.

One thing that icons like George insist on is taking time to learn as much about yourself, others, and the world as possible before attempting to influence it. George believes that when you do, you make yourself a much more valuable storyteller and professional as you start to develop your own ideas, values, and things that you want to say.

We should do the same. When we put in an abundant amount of preparation so that what we say becomes original (and not just a repeat of what others say), we can make a more powerful contribution to society than just by being in the echo chamber. Sure, this might take longer, but it will be worth it as our voices will be stronger and more influential.

SUMMARY: LIFE LESSONS FROM GEOGRE LUCAS

- The journey to success requires a willingness to be open to unexpected detours.
- Bigger goals come with bigger battles.
- Differentiate "kinda" cool from "absolutely necessary" to achieve true greatness.
- The highest calling of a leader is making others better.
- Developing your unique voice takes a lot of time.

"I think people who have faults are a lot more **interesting** than people who are perfect."

—Spike Lee

CHAPTER 35

SPIKE LEE

Spike Lee is the son of a teacher and jazz musician, and one of the first Black film directors to achieve mainstream success in America. As a director, writer, producer, and actor, he has helped showcase strong Black stories to the world using his artistic vision and creativity.

For example, Spike has helmed numerous films ranging from *Do The Right Thing* to *Malcolm X*, *BlackKKlansman* to *Da 5 Bloods*, and is the recipient of an Academy Award, 2 Emmy Awards, and 2 Peabody Awards, among other notable achievements. He has taught at Harvard University, and is a professor at the NYU Tisch School of the Arts, where he received his Master of Fine Arts degree.

SPIKE LEE'S TOP 5 LIFE LESSONS

> "I think it's very important that films make people look at what they've forgotten."

1. Remembering the best - and worst - of the past will help you become a better decision maker and an all-around better person.

The greatest film directors always look to the past to help their generation remember what came before them. And Spike certainly falls into this category.

For example, in the film *Malcolm X*, Spike wrote and directed the biopic of the iconic Black leader of the same name so that people could better understand the real-life Malcolm X's misunderstood identity (and learn from his successes and failures). Spike did the same thing when he brought to life the story of a Black police officer infiltrating the Ku Klux Klan to the movie *BlackKKlansman*, so we could learn how to better approach the racial tensions of the 21st Century.

The lesson we can learn here is that whether our chosen field is movies or anything else, we should look to see what came before us, as it will help us understand the world we're currently living in, and how we can best influence that world for the better.

> "I'm not going to let other people dictate to me who I should be or the stories I should tell."

2. If you never decide who you want to be, somebody else will try to do it for you.

One thing about Spike is that he is unapologetic about who he is. For example, he is a proud New Yorker, proud Knicks fan, and proud of telling Black stories.

However, not everyone appreciates that he focuses so much on his own culture and does not often venture outside of it. Many investors have passed on his projects, for example, because they were "too black" and felt that Spike's ideas could not reach mainstream audiences despite his prior successes. Nevertheless, Spike dismisses these people even if they offer him "less risky" projects that would require him to compromise on who he is or his vision of the world.

The takeaway from this is that even when we succeed, others still may doubt our vision and try to nudge us to become something we're not because it seems easier or safer. But Spike's example teaches us that we don't have to if we want to keep our integrity and be authentic to ourselves and our dreams.

> "It gets dangerous when you start allowing people to validate your work."

3. There will always be somebody who adores what you do - and somebody who absolutely abhors it too.

As strange as it sounds, Spike does not have a huge desire to get acclaim from others despite his numerous accomplishments. For example, even when film critics Siskel and Ebert ranked his movie *Do The Right Thing* as the best movie of 1989—and one of the best movies of the 1980s—Spike did not focus on trying to please them in his subsequent films.

To Spike, he believes you always have to believe in your own work and you should not become timid or less bold after you reach some modicum of success—a phenomenon that happens when people try to play it safe once they have a little bit of success and they're officially "in the club."

For you and me, there will be a strong desire to take less risks just to please others the more successful we become. However, if Spike can teach us anything, it is that the people who love our past work may not love our current or future work—and the people who hated our past work might love what we're working on now. As a consequence, we should not look to others for validation of what is in our hearts to do; we should just do it and let the chips fall where they may.

> "A lot of times we censor ourselves before the censor even gets there."

4. You are not called to stay quiet and blend in; you are called to be loud and stand out.

After the Academy of Motion Picture Arts and Sciences famously snubbed Spike's work for decades, Spike still did not back down in continuing to go after an Academy Award. And he did not back down doing it on his terms in his own style.

For example, when Spike won his first Oscar for penning *BlacKkKlansman* he wore a bright purple suit and jumped into Samuel Jackson's arms when his name was announced for the award—an antic that quickly broke the internet. But for Spike, he was simply being himself by writing the movie he wanted to write, wearing the suit he wanted to wear, and behaving how he wanted to behave.

The main lesson we can learn from this is that if we continue being ourselves, even if others do not recognize our greatness for a long time, they will eventually recognize it—and they will come to see just how unique we are, even if their eyes were previously closed to that uniqueness for a long time.

> "It's been my observation that parents kill more dreams than anybody."

5. Sometimes those closest to you will misunderstand why you were put on this earth.

As a college professor at the New York University Tisch School of the Arts, Spike comes into contact with countless students and parents, so he has an understanding of which kids are being supported and which kids aren't. And unfortunately, Spike has seen that some parents sometimes try to force their kids out of their dreams because they want them to play it safe—just like they did in their own lives.

But Spike is strongly against this approach. To him, if you have a dream, talent, and work very hard, you should pursue your dreams, even if your loved ones misunderstand you. And most artistically successful people would agree with him 1,000 percent.

SUMMARY: LIFE LESSONS FROM SPIKE LEE

- Remembering the best and worst of the past will make you a better person.
- Decide on who you want to be before someone else does.
- You will be both adored and abhorred by people in life.
- Accept your calling and don't be afraid to be loud and stand out.
- Even being misunderstood by those closest to you will happen from time to time.

"Curiosity is the most powerful thing you own."

—James Cameron

CHAPTER 36

JAMES CAMERON

James Cameron set the record for having not only the highest number of Academy Awards ever received (14), but also for having 2 of the highest grossing films of all time (*Titanic* and *Avatar*). And he did this by making original films in an era that preferred remakes and sequels.

As the writer-director of movies like *Terminator*, *Alien*, and *The Abyss*, James has experimented with genres, technologies, and new film approaches in a way almost no other director did before him. As a result, he has been named as one of the 100 Most Influential People in the world by *Time Magazine* and is considered arguably one of the most sophisticated technical directors in history.

But few people realize that prior to making it in movies, James was a janitor and truck driver who quit his job after seeing *Star Wars* because he was so mesmerized by its story and technology. Since this moment, James has directed countless films and become an outspoken advocate for environmental and vegan causes, and has opened up numerous ventures to help move the world in the direction of his profound new vision.

> "Don't put limitations on yourself. Others will do that for you."

1. Others can only stop you if you let them.

Although "just" a janitor and truck driver, James believed that he could make feature films even when others did not—and even when he had no experience in doing so. But because he had such a strong belief in himself, he was able to at least convince a few dentists to give him some "seed capital" so that he could start making films. (His first project wasn't a success, but it set the foundation for what was to come.)

In his early years, James realized that few others would encourage him to pursue his dreams and so he needed to encourage himself. In other words, he realized that he needed to get rid of negative thinking—or any preconceived limitations he put on himself—because he knew others would think negatively for him.

What you and I can learn from this is that, no matter who we are, there will be folks who do not recognize or understand the gifts and potential we have inside of us. And there will also be people that do recognize these things, but who nevertheless fear them, oppose them, or who are just too jealous or critical to support us as we reach toward our destinies. But despite this, they don't control our destinies, we do, so if we take the limits off of our thinking, we can truly take the limits off of our lives (even if others are trying desperately to put these limits back on).

> "Your only competitors are your past achievements."

2. Always believe your greatest days are ahead of you, not behind you.

After watching *Halloween* the movie in theaters, James was inspired, and so he went out and wrote the film *Terminator*. After Hollywood didn't get it and initially passed on the project, James found financing and made what would become one of the most iconic films of all time—and one of the most iconic film franchises.

But James didn't stop with *Terminator*. He also went on to make *Titanic*—which set the record for the highest grossing film of all time—before he broke his own record by releasing *Avatar*.

All throughout his life and career, James was always attempting to best his own past achievements with bigger and better ones. Whether bigger and better stories, technology, budgets, or revenues, James wanted to improve upon himself so that he could reach the greatness that he knew was within him. And so can we.

When we attempt to become better than we were before, we will always win because we will be growing into stronger and wiser versions of ourselves. It may not always be easy, but it will be worth it.

> "If you set your goals ridiculously high and it's a failure, you will fail above everyone else's success."

4. The only way you can be a player in the big leagues is if you aim to be.

Many people have criticized James because he is known to take off more than a decade between his big directorial projects. For example, he took off a decade between *Terminator 2* and *Terminator 3*, and he took off a decade between *Titanic* and *Avatar*. But James will tell you he needed that time off to develop the technology for his future projects so that they could match the vision he had in his mind.

Even though it would have been a lot easier to do easier projects with existing technology (and not take so much time off), James refused because he set his goals so high that he needed things to be done "right" (and not just easily). He needed to build a bigger pond for himself to fish in because he had outgrown the old pond.

What we can learn from this is that there will always be bigger ponds we can be swimming in (or building) regardless of if we think we have reached the pinnacle of our success. If we aim high, we are likely to succeed (even if we fail) as we will be in a stratosphere few others can even comprehend.

> "You have to not listen to the naysayers because there will be many and often they'll be much more qualified than you and cause you to sort of doubt yourself."

5. Even most successful people won't recognize your potential until you have achieved it.

Before becoming vegan was cool, James was an outspoken advocate for it. For example, he started the first vegan school with his wife as well as a large plant-based meat venture. He even made films about the environmental impacts of meat consumption and, consequently, ticked a lot of people off in the process.

James felt strongly that eating meat was an unnecessary—and unsustainable—choice people make, and he wanted to use every resource at his disposal to fight against these choices. Because he did, he was met with opposition—often from people much more credentialed and authoritative to speak on the subject than him—but he still forged ahead.

The takeaway here is that we will get doubters, haters, and critics not only because people disagree or disapprove of us; but we will get them because they don't think we're qualified or that we have the ability to pull off our vision. Regardless, though, we should move forward even if the smart naysayers don't believe in us until they see us reach our goals right in front of them.

SUMMARY: LIFE LESSONS FROM JAMES CAMERON

- Others can only stop you if you let them.
- Your greatest days are ahead of you.
- Meticulous decision-making will shape your future.
- Playing in the big leagues requires you to aim to play in the big leagues.
- Your potential will often go unrecognized until you have achieved it.

"Just because you are a **character** doesn't mean you have character."

—Quentin Tarantino

CHAPTER 37

QUENTIN TARANTINO

Quentin Tarantino is an Academy Award winning director whose feature films have earned him both a cult following and mainstream success. From *Kill Bill* to *Django Unchained*, *Pulp Fiction* to *Inglourious Basterds*, he has built a unique and iconic career that has allowed him to create his own "mini-universe of interconnected films."

Prior to becoming a director, though, Quentin worked a variety of roles to make ends meet. He was, for example, an Elvis impersonator, aerospace recruiter, and video store clerk before he was tapped for his directorial debut. Interestingly enough, as a video store clerk, people were astonished at his level of film knowledge which tipped them off that he was going to do great things with his life one day.

QUENTIN TARANTINO'S TOP 5 LIFE LESSONS

> "I want to top expectations. I want to blow you away."

1. Always give people a "wow factor."

   Quentin started off as an independent director, which meant that he had to look for ways to "impress" others in the Hollywood system before they took a chance on him. For example, he knew he had to create witty dialogue or dramatic action sequences (even on a limited budget) if he was to stand out and make a name for himself.

   But even though Quentin did this successfully in the beginning, he never lost the desire to blow you away throughout his legendary career. In every movie project he has ever taken on, for example, he has written and directed his films so that he could control the "wow factor." In other words, he wanted to make movies that were more than just derivative formulas meant to make easy money; he wanted to make movies that left you thinking, "wow, what did I just watch?"

   The takeaway for us is that we should seek to go above and beyond what is required of us in our work. But we should also seek to do this in our personal lives. When we consistently strive to be a great (and pleasurable) experience for others, our satisfaction—and theirs—will be immense.

> "I don't believe in elitism. I don't think the audience is this dumb person lower than me. I am the audience."

2. Greatness manifests when you recognize that you are neither superior or inferior to others.

At the age of 15, Quentin dropped out of high school to pursue other interests. He got into a bit of trouble, for example, by shoplifting at a Kmart, and did other things that did not set him up to be perceived as a future superstar filmmaker that he one day would become.

But his early experiences of being labeled a "dropout" and "criminal" also taught him to approach life—and his art—with a humility that is necessary to be a great storyteller. He didn't, for example, see himself as better than others, which helped him empathize with both the characters he created and his audiences. This empathy, in turn, is what would give him legend status because he could put himself in the shoes of those he was trying to make movies for (and understanding his audience was the key to his great success).

What you and I can learn from this is that to become great, we don't have to look down on or denigrate others. Even if we are extremely talented—and rich and popular and successful—if we reject unnecessary elitism we can be more sensitive to those around us and thus be better able to understand them—and make things for them that they'll love and voraciously consume.

> "Emotion will always win over coolness and cleverness."

3. People will reward you for a lifetime if you can take them on an emotional journey.

   Quentin is a huge fan of film, but a huge critic of film schools. For example, he has said that the best way to make movies is to watch them, not pay ample sums of money to learn clever ways to use a camera in a classroom. And he is on to something.

   Although school can be the right choice for some, it isn't for others, and Quentin recognized this for himself. He realized early on that to be a successful filmmaker, it wouldn't be about whether he could operate the latest and greatest technology; he realized that it would simply come down to being able to take audiences on an emotional journey that they would pay a high premium for.

   The same is true in your work. Whether you are in a creative field or not, the ability to move people's emotions (often using stories like Quentin) is what will help you reach superstar status as people will reward you when you can make them "feel" something.

> "It's my job to look at other people's humanity."

4. Never forget that all of the faces in the crowd are more than just anonymous statistics.

Although Quentin is among one of the most decorated filmmakers in history—multiple Oscars and Golden Globes, for example, as well as numerous Emmy and Grammy nominations—he doesn't let this get to his head. Or more specifically, he doesn't let it cause him to stop looking at other people's humanity (their hopes and dreams, their fears and concerns, and more). In other words, it is his ability to observe people—what they think, say, and do—and reinterpret that back to them that has made him an icon.

It is true that he is criticized for some of his artistic choices—as every filmmaker is—but he believes that he is simply creatively reflecting how people behave in real life in his work. And his work happens to feature the parts of people's humanity that isn't always so good.

The lesson here is that when we explore what makes people tick, we can find the truth that many people want to learn about themselves—and about society. And the only way we can do this is by being genuinely interested in human beings—both their good and their bad—and showing them who they truly are.

> "Personality goes a long way."

5. Showing your uniqueness carries greater rewards than you think.

Few people realize that Quentin was called to direct *Iron Man* as well as *Men in Black*, but ultimately did not do the projects. Although there are numerous reasons why this happened, part of the reason is because Quentin has always been best at allowing his personality to reflect in his original work—in his original stories—and not just the stories of others. And he has been rewarded handsomely for it.

For you and me, if we allow our unique personality to shine—especially at work—others will flock to us because they will be interested in how we see the world. Sure, some people might also not flock to us (because they don't like our personalities), but the right people will and it will be worth it to us by showing our most authentic selves.

SUMMARY: LIFE LESSONS FROM QUENTIN TARANTINO

- Wow people.
- Recognize you are neither superior or inferior to others.
- You will be rewarded if you take people on an emotional journey.
- The faces in the crowd amount to more than anonymous statistics.
- Your greatest rewards often come from showing your uniqueness.

"First, think. Second, believe. Third, dream. And finally, dare."

—Walt Disney

CHAPTER 38

WALT DISNE

Walt Disney was an entrepreneur, writer, producer, and prolific creator. Not only did he create *Mickey Mouse, Donald Duck, Snow White & The Seven Dwarfs*, and many other iconic franchises, but he also created Disneyland. And in the process, he picked up a record 22 Academy Awards, 3 Golden Globes, and an Emmy.

Walt got his start drawing horses on his uncle's ranch as a kid before becoming a cartoonist for his school newspaper and putting himself through art school at night. After a series of failures and missteps, he founded what would become The Walt Disney company, which would become one of the most dominant entertainment companies in history.

WALT DISNEY'S TOP 5 LIFE LESSONS

> "Imagination has no age. Dreams are forever."

1. You will never outgrow your dreams.

Walt's last name—Disney—has become synonymous with fun, imagination, and child-like wonder. Because to him, life was about releasing the inner-child in every person.

For example, every character, movie, and television show Walt created, he created for two audiences in mind: kids and adults. Although it would seem that his content like *Cinderella* and *Mary Poppins* were only aimed at children, Walt's real aim was something that kids and parents could enjoy together (a strategy Pixar would adopt decades later). And the reason he did this was because Walt wanted multiple generations to escape into the dream life they had always imagined.

The takeaway here is that no matter how old we are, not only do we have dreams in us, but we have child-like dreams. And Walt would want us to indulge in these types of dreams not just as a form of entertainment, but as a way of life. He never stopped believing in the child-like dreams he had as a kid—and because he did this, he gave others' permission to start believing in their own child-like dreams too.

> "All you've got to do is own up to your ignorance honestly, and you'll find people who are eager to fill your head with information."

2. The more humble you are about your own limitations, the more others will want to help you.

Walt Disney was not only a life-long entrepreneur, but he was a life-long learner and experimenter. It started with him taking art classes at night and on weekends to improve his own artistic skills, but then it became something much bigger later in his life.

For example, he realized that most of his animators were trained in a particular type of animation, but that they didn't know much more beyond that. And he believed that their lack of knowledge—and their lack of training—would not allow them to create a future beyond their own current technological boundaries and limitations. So, he decided to set up a school for them— now called "CalArts"—so that they could continue learning regardless of how much knowledge or success they had before enrolling in that school.

The lesson here is that no matter who we are—or what we have achieved—we can always get better. The more we recognize (and accept) this, the easier it will be for us to continue learning things we don't know so that we can confidently march into the future.

> "That's the trouble with the world, too many people grow up. They forget."

3. When life becomes about chores and not fun, it's too late.

Although Walt's job was to have fun, it wasn't destined to be. He had to create a fun job—and a fun company and fun reality for himself—so that he could do this. Because, at heart, he was a big kid who felt that people become too serious and lost in their to-do list the older they get. As a consequence, he believed that not only are they not having fun, but they're missing out on the most magical parts of their lives.

To counter this, Walt wanted to create "the happiest place on earth"—Disneyland—so that, at least for a moment, people could be kids again. However, not everyone was so keen about this. For example, even the adults on Walt's board of directors were skeptical to support his dream amusement park—they were too busy "adulting"—so Disney did not ask them to support him. Instead, he personally paid for Disneyland himself (even putting his own home on the line to have enough money to pay construction workers) just so that he could provide a space for people to be happy.

For you and me, we should see that we should never outgrow fun. Even if we are in a "serious" or "challenging" profession, having fun will be key to enjoying ourselves. Of course, it doesn't mean we should shirk our responsibilities, but it does mean we should regularly program fun into our daily lives so that life doesn't become an endless to-do list.

> "We keep moving forward, opening new doors, and doing new things, because we're curious and curiosity keeps leading us down new paths."

4. Curiosity is the first step toward changing the world—or, at least, changing your world.

Because Walt financed Disneyland himself, he needed to figure out how to offer rides and experiences to people they had never had before. And he did this not because it was simply a business strategy; he did this because it was an artistic imperative that was born out of his own deep curiosity about what "might be." Instead of accepting the status quo like so many others, he let his imagination take him for a ride into the future—and then he made that future a reality.

The lesson here is that the more we ask ourselves "why aren't things different?" or "why can't they be done this way instead of that way?" the more we will blaze new trails and conquer new territory. Of course, many people around us will not want us to ask these questions, but we don't have to let them stop us.

> "We are not trying to entertain the critics. I'll take my chances with the public."

5. Do not live your life for the haters—they will hate you no matter what.

Despite receiving 22 Academy Awards, many people questioned Walt. They questioned his characters, for example, along with his storylines and business decisions. And they questioned almost everything else about him.

Nevertheless, Walt knew that to become great, you had to go through the Valley of the Haters. But he also knew that the haters had no power to stop you from reaching your dreams if you didn't give them any power to stop you.

What we can learn from him is that we do not need to make our products, services, or life decisions to satisfy those who are just looking to troll or question us; we need to make these things first for ourselves and second for the people who will appreciate all that we have to offer. When we do this, haters will fade into the dust where they belong.

SUMMARY: LIFE LESSONS FROM WALT DISNEY

- Never outgrow your dreams.
- Humility about your limitations will draw others to help you.
- It's too late when you bog down your life in chores and not fun.
- The first step to changing the world is curiosity.
- Haters will hate you no matter what so there is no need to try to impress them or prove them wrong..

"It's fun doing something that hasn't been done before."

—Stan Lee

CHAPTER 39

STAN LEE

Stan Lee was a comic book writer and the creative director of Marvel Entertainment for decades. He created the beloved characters Spiderman, Iron Man, Thor, Black Panther, The X-Men, Captain Marvel, and many others. And he helped turn his characters into the most dominant movie and television franchises to ever grace Hollywood.

But growing up, Stan was not immersed in a creative or wealthy environment. His dad was a dress cutter, for example, and Stan himself wrote obituaries and delivered sandwiches just to make ends meet weekly. But still he had a desire to write and create, which led him to Marvel and eventually to becoming an icon and legend.

STAN LEE'S TOP 5 LIFE LESSONS

> "I don't have inspiration. I only have ideas. Ideas and deadlines."

1. To become great, you do not need to wait for inspiration to get started.

Stan Lee was as prolific a writer and creator as they come. For example, he created over 300 characters in his time—and over 60 superheroes. But he also wrote endless comic books for these heroes, bringing his total output to an immeasurable amount.

However, whenever people asked Stan how he got inspired to write as much as he did, he gave them an answer they were not expecting: he simply wrote. That is, he did not wait to feel "inspired" to write. Nor did he wait until his circumstances were ideal. He simply wrote and wrote and wrote some more.

The lesson we can take away from this is that to become prolific, we do not need to feel like doing something. We just have to do it. And the more we do it, the easier it will become so that we can simply create or produce on demand regardless of how we're feeling or what our circumstances are (as if creating or producing is second nature to us, because it will be).

> "I don't really see a need to retire as long as I'm having fun."

2. Do not create a life you want to retire from.

After Stan Lee stepped down from running Marvel Entertainment in the 90s, he didn't simply enter retirement. Sure, he had the title "Chairman Emeritus" and still drew a salary of over $1 million dollars a year, but he didn't stop creating.

For example, Stan set up a new company so that he could continue to create more and more characters outside of the Marvel brand. To him, creating wasn't simply to get rich, famous, or become iconic; it was something that he had to do, and something that he never wanted to stop doing.

For you and me, what we can learn is that we should choose a career—or careers—that we will want to pursue forever. Of course, this might be difficult if you're still deciding on your interests and passions (particularly if you are young), but once you figure it out, it will help you do the things that you love to do (and will never want to stop doing).

> "Every day is a new adventure."

3. You can find magic when you look for it.

Stan was only 17 years old when he got hired in his first comic book role. But he wasn't hired to be a fancy writer or head development. Instead, he was hired for something much more humbling.

For example, Stan came on board to do menial tasks around the office, like making sure ink was available for pens (in his day, ink wells were the standard writing instruments). Over time, though, he was able to make his way up the corporate ladder because he always kept a positive attitude and saw his job as magical. And it was this ability to see his time as an adventure that put him in position to not only withstand the early humbling years, but also to keep himself hungry to create characters for decades to come.

The lesson here is that no matter what your job is—or where you start—if you look at what you do with awe, it will make it so much more special. Even if you are low on the totem pole at the moment, choose to view your job with wonder as it will put you in a position to unleash the hidden talents that are within you.

> "I used to be embarrassed because I was just a comic book writer while other people were building bridges or going on to medical careers. And then I began to realize: entertainment is one of the most important things in people's lives. Without it, they might go off on the deep end."

4. Always remember no matter what you do, it is just as important as what others are doing too.

Stan became a comic book writer during a time of great distress in the world. For example, the world was experiencing depression and war and he felt an obligation to do "serious things."

So, he entered the army and did what he could to contribute, but still his desire to write comic books was stronger than serving in any other way.

What Stan realized is that everyone is called to do and be something that is right for them, even if it isn't right for others. Of course, not everyone will see it that way (even Stan changed his name on the cover of Marvel magazines to conceal his identity from his friends who thought comic book writing was superfluous). But, over time, Stan learned to publicly embrace that his profession—his calling—was just as important as that of a medical doctor or great general.

For you and me, what we can recognize from this is that accepting who we truly are is the first step to greatness. Even if friends, family, or society don't recognize it immediately, we should know that what we chose to do matters and is needed in the world (and we should never let anyone make us believe otherwise).

> "No one has a perfect life. Everyone has something that he wishes was not the way it is."

5. Perfection only exists in fairy tales.

Like other icons and legends, Stan was a very wealthy man. Some estimates even had his fortune north of $50 million dollars. However, that did not mean everything was peachy for him.

For example, Stan felt like he was not being adequately compensated by Fox and Sony when the first *X-Men* and *Spiderman* movies came out, so he had to pursue litigation against them. Even though he didn't want to do this—and even though they were making billions of dollars off of his creation—he felt he was being treated unfairly, so he did everything he could to protect himself. (He won a settlement, by the way, and was able to be appropriately paid for his creations.)

The takeaway for us is that regardless of the level of success that will come to our lives, our circumstances won't always be perfect. And not even fame or fortune can bail us out of this basic reality. However, if we begin to see that life has its up moments and down moments, we will appreciate the up moments so much more.

SUMMARY: LIFE LESSONS FROM STAN LEE

- Don't wait for inspiration to strike if you are seeking greatness.
- Create a life you don't want to retire from.
- When you look for it, you will find magic.
- What you do, and what others do, are both important.
- Only fairy tales have perfection.

PART IV
TALK SHOW HOSTS

No list of icons and legends would be complete without Hollywood's trailblazing talk show hosts. These hosts—ranging from Oprah Winfrey to Larry King, Tyra Banks to Steve Harvey and beyond—have come into America's living rooms not only to entertain, but often to inform, inspire, and empower.

Like the other icons from the entertainment industry, our talk show hosts have overcome incredible odds in their lives that make them seem almost superhuman—which makes their soulful advice all the more powerful.

Although many people would be dismissive of advice from talk show hosts, the reality is that we have much to learn from their ability to reach into our emotional and social realities and help us make sense of ourselves—and the world around us.

Now, let's dig deeper into the people often known as America's pop psychologists.

"The great courageous act that we must all do is have the **courage** to step out of our history and past so we can live our dreams."

—Oprah

CHAPTER 40

OPRAH WINFREY

Oprah Winfrey is an 18x Emmy, Tony, and Peabody award-winning television talk show host who re-invented the field of daytime television. And when she did it, not only did she become the richest African American woman in the world, but she also became the most influential woman of any ethnic background in the entire century.

Through television shows, book clubs, magazines, movies, and other game-changing endeavors, Oprah has defined media for an entire generation and helped launch the careers of countless successful individuals and organizations. And she did this all despite coming from a deeply impoverished and traumatized background. Her incredible rise to the top taught her many timeless lessons that you can use any time in your life.

OPRAH'S TOP LIFE LESSONS

"Turn your wounds into wisdom."

1. No matter who you are, life will present you with one all-defining choice: to become bitter OR become better as a result of the wounds other people and circumstances have caused you.

   As a child, Oprah was molested, and as a result she gave birth to a son at age 14. But unfortunately, her son died, which left her devastated and with an unbelievably difficult choice to make: to choose between letting her loss and pain "define" her OR letting her loss and pain "refine" her. Fortunately for her—and for the world—she chose the latter.

   Oprah decided early in life to use her hurts, wounds, setbacks, and obstacles to strategically propel her to greater and greater heights because she chose to react positively and not negatively to them. Each time she chose to "look on the bright side" when her world tumbled down around her, for example, she was able to more easily conquer future pain that tried to stop her from being the best version of herself—and from reaching her goals and living her dreams.

   For you and me, we will also face the same choice of deciding to be "victims" OR "overcomers" through various negative circumstances we will inevitably face in life. If we choose to be overcomers—which I believe we should—we will become unstoppable just like Oprah because we will be making our souls resilient to setbacks.

> "Every time you suppress some part of yourself or allow others to play you small, you are ignoring the owner's manual your Creator gave you."

2. You don't have to live in the boxes other people try to force you in.

Although daytime talk shows were considered "tabloid television" in the 1980s when she started, Oprah refused to let this label stick to her. In fact, she decided that she would re-define the talk show format to include spirituality, social causes, and a variety of other factors people said would never work. Of course, her way worked and other people's so-called "advice" disappeared like dust.

The takeaway for Oprah was that other people will always try to tell you what is "right," what is "best," how you "should" live, but in reality you have to resist living in the limited sandcastle they want you to live your life in. Instead, you should build your own castle—a real castle, made of real substance—and live there even if people think you are foolish for not abiding by the rules they have arbitrarily set for your life.

> "Everyone is keeper of a dream."

3. God gives you a dream that only you are qualified to bring into existence.

Oprah believes that everyone is given a dream, a talent, or a gift that only they are capable of using for the greater good. For her, her dream was to help heal people's souls through the power of positive television and speaking hope and encouragement into homes daily. But this was a risk. After all, most other daytime television was trashy at the time, but Oprah knew she could be different—and better.

Even though she was looked upon as strange for wanting to bring spirituality into television, for example, she felt because it was a dream in her heart that she had to do it regardless of how it "made her look." And so she did.

In your life, you are the steward of something special that can make a powerful impact in the lives of others if only you will take small steps of courage daily to release it, no matter how hard it is for you, or how weird it appears to others.

> "You don't become what you want, you become what you believe."

4. Your beliefs are powerful enough to rearrange your circumstances.

The world often operates by the motto of "I'll believe it when I see it." However, Oprah does just the opposite: she sees it in her mind's eye, and then she believes it. In other words, Oprah has cultivated a mindset for herself that allows her to "see" things before they are real, and as a consequence create "self-fulfilling prophecies."

For example, Oprah will often have a vision for an interview or television show or movie and, before she knows it, it becomes a reality. And it doesn't just become reality because she has the money and power to make it happen; even when she had no money and no power, for example, she saw things before they happened and worked "backwards" to make sure they were brought to life.

For you and me, if we embrace the fact that we have to have a vision for who we are—and for what we can do—before we become or do these things, we can accomplish more of our goals than we realize. We just have to have more faith in ourselves and not just "see what happens" and "go with the flow" as so many people tend to do.

> "When I look to the future it is so bright it burns my eyes!"

5. If you chase the future you will eventually catch it.

When Oprah thinks about what is ahead of her, it ignites so much passion that she doesn't remember what is behind her. Put differently, Oprah has learned that the secret to success is always envisioning a better future for yourself and reaching toward it. For her, whether that is the next book or next show or next movie, she is constantly imagining what could be, which keeps life fresh and interesting.

For you, if you continuously think about the new and exciting things you can do—and, more importantly, the new and exciting person you can grow into in the coming months and years— you will wake up with so much joy and energy that you will know that your tomorrows will be greater than your yesterdays (and there's nothing better than that).

SUMMARY: LIFE LESSONS FROM OPRAH WINFREY

- Life always presents the choice of becoming bitter or better.
- Live outside of the boxes people attempt to put you in.
- Only you are qualified to bring into existence the dream that God gave you.
- Powerful beliefs can rearrange your circumstances.
- Chase your future and your will eventually catch it.

"A man cannot be made to feel uncomfortable without his own approval."

—Barbara Walters

CHAPTER 41

BARBARA WALTERS

Barbara Walters is a journalist and television personality who has served as host of *20/20*, *The View*, and the *ABC Evening News* among many other programs. Her awards include 2 daytime Emmy Awards, an NAACP Image Award, and numerous other accolades that have spanned a 70 year career.

She is the daughter of refugees who came to America to seek a better life, and had siblings who battled mental illness for decades. Barbara's adventures in media would eventually earn her legions of fans—and arguably the title of the greatest female journalist of all time.

BARBARA WALTER'S TOP 5 LIFE LESSONS

"Fight the big fight, don't fight the little fight."

1. The size of your battles determines the size of your rewards.

Because Barbara is the daughter of a nightlife promoter, she was around numerous celebrities and influential figures growing up. As a consequence, she was exposed to not only the upsides and downsides of this, but also to how larger-than-life figures thought and conducted themselves in their business affairs.

For example, Barbara's dad used his nightclub influence to become a Broadway producer which put Barbara in the presence of some of the biggest performers in New York City. She had a front row seat to people like Florenz Ziegfeld (a legendary theater performer) and she learned from him (and others) that you truly have to fight in order to make your big dreams come true. But she also learned that you have to fight to make your little dreams come true too, so you might as well fight for the big things in life because either way you will be spending your limited time battling for something you want.

The takeaway from this is that whenever we have multiple goals in life, we should choose the bigger goals to go after because we will have to fight as much for the bigger goals as we do the little goals—so we might as well choose the big ones with our limited time on the earth.

> "A big laugh makes any interview, any conversation, so much better."

2. Loosening up a bit will multiply your friendships.

Barbara interviewed everyone from President Richard Nixon to popstar Michael Jackson. In all of her numerous discussions, she learned that she should incorporate laughter not just to break the ice, but all throughout her conversations.

But Barbara also did this in her personal life. She was, for example, good friends with comedians like Woody Allen who showed her that it was okay to keep things light and fun—even in the midst of serious interviews, difficult personal circumstances, and any other possible scenario in life. Because she adopted this, she was able to develop a personal and professional rolodex of people she could call friends (and whom she could count on at various points in her life).

For you and me, what we can learn is that it is okay to let down our guard with people. We do not need to be perfect or always put together to succeed with them, and we do not have to always be so serious either. If we lighten up a bit, we might be surprised how many people appreciate our fun approach to life (and allow us to get close to them).

> **"The hardest thing you will ever do is trust yourself."**

3. Believing in yourself starts with accepting that you are not an accident.

   Barbara is truly a trailblazer in the media. She was one of the first female anchors of a major television news show, and she was also one of the creators of a major ensemble talk show (*The View*) that had never been attempted before. And every time she went on air, she had to learn to trust herself with these endeavors.

   For example, because nobody who looked like her had ever done what she did before, that meant that she had to take an enormous leap of faith on herself, especially in the early days. Many men did not like this (they thought she was too big for her britches). Nevertheless, she learned to trust herself over time—through many successes and some failures—which gave her confidence to continue in her career.

   The lesson here is trusting ourselves—both personally and professionally—will be something we have to learn to do over and over again. Because we will experience not only self-doubt at times, but also experience critics, haters, and naysayers, we must learn to develop tiny amounts of confidence in ourselves no matter what we are feeling (or what others are saying). And once we have these tiny bits of confidence, we can grow them bit by bit until we are oozing with so much confidence and charisma we can hardly stand ourselves.

> "Personal gain is empty if you do not feel you have positively touched another's life."

4. No real success means anything unless you have lifted up others along the way.

Although Barbara is responsible for conducting the most-watched interview of all time—her interview with Monica Lewinsky that aired to more than 75 million people in real time—along with many other successes, she doesn't believe any of it would mean anything unless she has helped others succeed. And this is one of the reasons why she has created content meant to inspire and uplift, not just entertain.

For example, few people realize Barbara started off as a children's television producer—which allowed her to inspire kids—before moving on to featuring stories that would also inspire adults. But Barbara did this because it was important to her to make a powerful and positive impact on others not just through philanthropy, but with the work she did day in and day out.

Our lesson is that in all that we do, we should create ways to help, encourage, and inspire others. From family to friends, coworkers to community members—and beyond—we should use our success to make other people's lives better. Nothing will be more rewarding than that, absolutely nothing.

> "Success can go one of two ways. It can make you a prima donna—or it can smooth the edges, take away the insecurities, let the nice things come out."

5. **Success, more than failure, will reveal who you are underneath.**

Most people think that success changes people. But not Barbara. She actually believes that success reveals who people always have been—for better or for worse.

In her own life, for example, she has believed success has played a role in helping her become a better person, even though she's also seen it tear apart many lives too.

For you and me, we should not be afraid of achieving success because of how it might change us because the reality is it will likely only reveal who we already are. So, if we work on our characters before we reach the mountaintop, we will have something good to hold onto once we get there.

SUMMARY: LIFE LESSONS FROM BARBARA WALTERS

- The size of your rewards is often equal to or greatly surpasses the size of your battles.
- Multiply your friendships by loosening up a bit.
- Accept that you are not an accident.
- Capture true success by lifting up others along the way.
- Success reveals your true character.

"I never learned [anything] while I was talking."

—Larry King

CHAPTER 42

LARRY KING

Larry King was an Emmy and Peabody Award winning journalist and commentator whose career spanned over 50 years. He conducted more than 50,000 interviews during his lifetime and set a Guinness Book of World Records as the host of his famed *Larry King Live* show on CNN.

Prior to becoming a media hit, however, he grew up as the son of a poor garment worker and was raised on welfare in New York. The reality of living in poverty caused him to work to escape it, and contributed to his legendary work ethic that led to his working all the way until his passing in 2021 (in his 80s).

LARRY KING'S TOP 5 LIFE LESSONS

> "If you do something, expect consequences."

1. When you do things that winners do, you will win.

   From an early age, Larry wanted to go into media as a way to move beyond his poverty-stricken upbringing. So, when he learned that Florida was a training ground for young, inexperienced journalists, he immediately moved there from Brooklyn to put himself in a position to succeed. And he did.

   For example, he started to work at a local radio station in Miami and, when the main on-air announcer unexpectedly quit, Larry was given his spot. From then on, Larry used his very small platform as an opportunity to leverage what he could gain, namely more experience and exposure so he could, step by step, reach his dreams. In other words, Larry knew that he could expect good consequences for himself if he kept doing the right things (even if the right things were as extreme as moving thousands of miles away from home just to take on a small opportunity he couldn't have gotten elsewhere).

   What we can learn from this is there are always consequences to our actions as it relates to our success. Whether we take small steps—or extreme ones—toward our goals, something positive will happen for us so long as we don't quit. And if we take enough steps in the right direction, we will win consistently because that is what winners do.

> "You cannot talk to people successfully if you are not interested in what they have to say or you have no respect for them."

2. The best conversationalists are truly curious about what others are telling them.

   Larry was known for his direct, non-confrontational interview style. This allowed him to interview everyone from UFO conspiracy theorists to psychics to world class athletes and heads of state. But regardless of who he was interviewing, he always took interest in who his guests were, what they wanted to say, and then gave them an opportunity to say it.

   For example, he had leaders on his show like George W. Bush and Al Gore who he gave an opportunity to explain themselves—without trying to trick them, make them look bad, or use them to make himself look better (an approach that would become more common in cable television years later). And Larry did this because he genuinely respected them as human beings and wanted them to get out their message without his filter interfering with them. Because he did this, he was able to interview thousands of people from all walks of life over a 50 year span because people trusted him—and respected him too.

   The takeaway from this is that in both our personal and professional lives, if we respect others and are curious about what they're telling us, they will likely reward us by trusting us and respecting us too. But we can't wait for them to initiate this trust and respect; we must initiate it ourselves before they will reciprocate.

> "Getting your house in order and reducing the confusion gives you more control over your life. Personal organization somehow releases or frees you to operate more effectively."

3. A successful life is usually an organized one.

The older Larry got the more he believed in the simplicity of life—and in the simplicity of organizing his life. He, for example, kept things tidy at home and maintained a regular daily routine at his local bagel shop so that he could reduce uncertainty in his life.

By being so organized and structured personally, Larry believed that he was in a better position professionally because his mind was free from unnecessary uncertainty. As simple as it sounds, he believed even a small amount of order in his house and daily routine could produce big results in his career. And he was right.

The lesson that Larry shows—which many other icons and legends have adopted—is that being disciplined, organized, and structured at home allows them to dominate at work because they have less things to focus on that could potentially distract them.

> "There is nothing in your destiny, nothing in your future that you cannot accomplish."

4. Achieving something - small or great - starts with believing that you can.

Even though Larry was known for interviewing others, he was also quite the actor and writer. For example, he acted in movies ranging from *Ghostbusters* to *Shrek*, and shows ranging from *The People vs. OJ Simpson* to *Law in Order*.

But Larry didn't stop in his pursuit of only "mainstream" success or ventures. He even acted in numerous infomercials because he had diversified interests and goals outside of his show *Larry King Live*. And Larry did these things because he believed he could accomplish anything he put his mind to.

What you and I can learn from this is that if you have goals and passions—even if they're outside of your career or main areas of strength—you can still succeed in those if you simply believe that you can. Sure, it might take some time, training, and relentless persistence, but that is all it will take. And aren't your desires worth a bit of investment?

> "Even those who have a natural ability for something have to work to develop it."

5. Turning your natural talent into skill through discipline is the quickest path to greatness.

Larry had a natural talent for interviewing people. But he had to work hard at it, and he had to interview countless people before he could be comfortable enough talking to them without notes or preconceived questions beforehand.

In his first job as a radio personality in Miami, for example, he would interview anybody who was willing to come on the air—a local waitress, a guy he saw on the sidewalk, anyone really. And he did this because he knew he needed the practice. Of course, this worked out for him because thousands of interviews later he was regularly landing the biggest celebrities and heads of state of all time on his show (because he was a practiced pro).

For you and me, we might have some talent at something but if we work at it over and over again we can truly become a master of it. And once we become a master of it, we can put ourselves in position to truly unleash the greatness that is within us.

SUMMARY: LIFE LESSONS FROM LARRY KING

- To win, do what winners do.
- Generate great conversation by showing genuine curiosity about others.
- Organize your life to achieve the best success.
- Achievement starts with strong self-belief.
- The quickest path to greatness is by sharpening your talent into disciplined skill.

"Never dull your shine for **somebody** else."

—Tyra Banks

CHAPTER 43

TYRA BANKS

Tyra Banks is one of the most iconic models of all time. With a net worth hovering around $100 .million dollars, Tyra has parlayed her covergirl status from Sports Illustrated to running her own shows like The Tyra Banks Show and America's Next Top Model.

Tyra was born in Inglewood, California, and was called an "ugly duckling" by classmates who thought that she was "too fat" and had a "big forehead." Nevertheless, that did not stop her from beginning to model at age 15 and becoming a Victoria's Secret Angel and "Supermodel of the Year" within a few short years after that.

She has written multiple New York Times Bestselling books, won two Emmy Awards, attended Harvard University, and been a lecturer at Stanford University. And she's done all of these things not only to live up to her potential, but to help other people live up to theirs (particularly young African American girls who she feels need more role models).

TYRA BANKS TOP LIFE LESSONS

> "Perfect is boring, human is beautiful"

1. To become an icon, realness must be valued over perfection.

Although Tyra came to fame gracing the covers of *Elle*, *Vogue*, *Cosmopolitan*, and walking the fashion runways of Chanel, Dior, and Calvin Klein, she doesn't believe that looks are everything. In fact, she believes it is her personality—who she is on the inside—that allowed her to leverage her success as a model and turn herself into an icon.

For example, Tyra used her down to earth personality to impress casting directors to give her a small role on the hit show *The Fresh Prince of Bel Air*. From there, she got bigger roles in movies like *Coyote Ugly* and translated her on-air success into becoming the creator and host of *America's Next Top Model*. In other words, Tyra was able to use her realness as a person to get her into places—as an actress or television host—that her looks could not have kept her in the long run.

What we can learn from this is that being ourselves—instead of trying to live up to a pretend perfect standard people try to impose on us—will help us win in the long run so long as we don't sell out our "realness" for society's "fakeness."

> "I became the victim of myself."

2. **Your own negative thoughts and behaviors can harm you more than you realize.**

Because Tyra started off as a model and an actress, she was used to constantly being judged for her looks, sense of style, and every waking movement. As a consequence, she became not only very self-conscious, but she also became self-critical in that she would harshly criticize herself and her own looks for not being the "perfect" model everyone wanted her to be. But she didn't let this self-critical attitude defeat her in the long run.

When Tyra got her own show, for example, she decided to host an episode on cellulite so that she—and other women—could have a candid conversation on the reality of body image. By just being able to talk about the "perceived flaws" that society tries to belittle women with was healing and cathartic for her—and for millions across the country.

What we can learn from this is that we don't have to let our own negative thoughts cause emotional storms inside of us by trying to live up to unrealistic standards of other people. Instead, we can stop criticizing ourselves and our own perceived flaws so that we can live healthier, more empowered lives—after all, we gain nothing by mistreating ourselves.

> "You've got to learn to accept the fool in you, as well as the part that's got it goin' on."

3. Every person has an Aristotle and Homer Simpson inside of them.

Though many people think that a supermodel as sophisticated and successful as Tyra Banks is should have it all together, the reality is that Tyra embraces her goofy side. And the results are spectacular.

For example, Tyra once "fake" passed out on an episode of *America's Next Top Model* just to get a reaction out of that season's competitors. To their shock, after Tyra hit the floor and they checked her pulse, she surprised them that it was just a joke to see how they would respond.

In our own lives, we can also embrace our fun sides and sense of humor. In fact, research shows that the more we joke and laugh, the stronger our physical, mental, and emotional health will be, so we should prioritize this aspect of our lives like Tyra.

> "There's always going to be dreams and goals I have, but I never really tell people what they are."

4. People need to earn the right to know the plans you have for your future.

Growing up in urban Los Angeles, a lot of people would frown upon the dreams and goals Tyra had because they thought they were unattainable. In their view, they couldn't believe that a Black girl from the hood could possibly be on the cover of major fashion magazines and become a dominant television personality.

As a result of this experience, Tyra learned that she didn't need to run around and tell everyone what she was planning to do. Not only was this a logical approach—it would prevent her from having to hear the thoughts of naysayers and doubters—but it helped her to protect her greatest ideas in Hollywood. For example, as the creator of *America's Next Top Model*, she was able to protect the idea of the show from being stolen by better known Hollywood figures until she was in a position to make it happen herself.

What we can take away from this is that we can quietly pursue our dreams without having to announce to everyone our strategic plan for conquering the world. This will help limit negative people who could rise up against us as well as reduce potential threats on the path to securing our goals.

> "There's no excuse for rudeness."

5. No matter how important, successful, busy, distracted, angry, or hurt you are, if you prioritize being kind to others you will always be a winner in life.

One of the biggest misconceptions about Hollywood or being a celebrity is that everyone who is involved in the entertainment industry is somehow rude or stuck up. But Tyra learned that, while there might be some people who are snobs, the reality is they are few and far between and that it is the genuinely nice and helpful people who advance the quickest—and stay on top the longest—in Tinseltown.

The lesson here is that not only is it good manners not to be rude to others, it is also strategic and beneficial to your career if you exhibit kindness to those around you.

SUMMARY: LIFE LESSONS FROM TYRA BANKS

- To become an icon, you must value realness over perfection.
- Negativity in your thoughts and behaviors will crucify you.
- There is an Aristotle and a Homer Simpson that lives within all of us.
- Others have to qualify themselves to learn about the plans for your future.
- Prioritizing being king will always make you a winner in life.

"Your career is what you're paid for. Your calling is what you're made for."

—Steve Harvey

CHAPTER 44

STEVE HARVEY

Steve Harvey is one of the most inspirational—and iconic—entertainers of all time. Not only is he a 6x Emmy Award Winner and 14x NAACP Image Award Winner, but he overcame many years of homelessness, showering at gas stations, and other hardships to rise to where he is today.

For example, starting off as a young comedian, he worked odd jobs as a carpet cleaner and mechanic just to make enough money to travel to perform at low-paying stand-up comedy clubs (but not enough money to afford to stay in an apartment or even a cheap motel). But after 3 years of doing this, things turned around for Steve and the rest is history.

For example, he has starred in *The Steve Harvey Show*, hosted *Family Feud* and *Showtime* at the *Apollo*, performed in *The Original Kings of Comedy*, and has been a bestselling author and big time movie producer, including creating hits like *Think Like a Man*.

STEVE HARVEY'S TOP 5 LIFE LESSONS

> "Your dream has to be bigger than your fear."

1. Imaginary obstacles kill more dreams than real ones do.

   If anyone had reasons to doubt his dreams, it was Steve. He worked in low-paying jobs and was homeless for years, for example, and nobody believed he could become an "everyday success" much less an iconic one.

   But despite his circumstances and the lack of belief of the people around him, Steve still believed that the only obstacle that could stop him wasn't outside of him; he believed the only obstacle that could stop him was inside of him. So, he decided he wouldn't let his own negative thoughts hold him back from pursuing his heart's desire because he knew he had a gift that would one day change his circumstances - and one day change the doubt of those around him.

   In our own lives, we should recognize that any negative temporary circumstances we find ourselves in—and any lack of support from others toward us—is not enough to stop us from going after what we want if we are determined to. If we eliminate all excuses about the real and imaginary obstacles in our way, we can achieve more than we ever dreamed of just like Steve.

2. If your dream is important enough, it will override any hesitation in pursuing it.

In retrospect, it always seems like iconic superstars like Steve never faced fear or self-doubt but nothing could be further from the truth. Although he has a net worth north of $200 million dollars, he only got it because he decided to take his fears head on.

For example, Steve experienced so many fears that would stop most dead in their tracks. From being called a failure to rejection after rejection in auditions to financial and housing instability, Steve's early years were a case study in "if something can go wrong, it will." But regardless of these things, Steve felt he was destined to have his name in lights and so he was willing to endure any hardship to get there.

The takeaway here is that we must be willing to walk through the nightmare part of a dream to reach its ultimate blessings. If for any reason we are not bold enough to do this, most of us will give up on our dreams—and give up on ourselves—before we ever begin our journeys.

> "Your mission, your purpose, and your destiny will all be tied to one thing - your gift."

3. The minute you discover and embrace your gift is the minute your destiny begins.

Steve knew he was good at making people laugh. And the minute he recognized this his own hero's journey began.

For example, Steve started performing in extremely small comedy clubs and, with each experience, honed his skills to become better and better—and funnier and funnier. By the time he launched the most successful and profitable comedy tour of all time—The Original Kings of Comedy Tour—he was skillful and funny enough to consistently live his purpose night after night.

What is interesting about this for you and me is that even though Steve had a gift early on, he still had to work very hard to improve it and go through many ups and downs before he ultimately became successful in his life's work. In our own lives, we will have to see that our gift can allow us to be out of this world successful, but only if we are willing to put in the time and sacrifice so that we can use it regularly and leverage it to our advantage.

> "Stop wasting time looking at somebody else's reality while doing nothing about yours."

4. Tearing others down will never lift you up.

When Steve hosted the 2015 Miss Universe contest, he accidentally called the name of the 2nd place winner—Miss Columbia—which caused him to be mocked endlessly online and in television outlets. What Steve learned from this experience is that many of the people who were mocking him had not done much of anything with their own lives, which helped him more easily dismiss their attacks.

The takeaway from this experience is that even if we stumble and fall in the pursuit of our dreams, we are in a better position than those who only want to point out our mistakes but never do anything significant with their own lives.

> "When you're happy at home, you can make a lot of things happen."

5. Strongly investing in your family life will not only bring personal benefits, but also professional benefits too.

Steve credits his third wife Marjorie for helping to turn around his life. Even though he had fame and fortune before meeting her, for example, he believes she was the person who brought more peace, joy, and stability into his life than anyone or anything before that. And as a consequence, Steve credit's his personal transformation to her (and her sharing her deep Christian faith with him, which he adopted).

Today, Steve's career has exploded to an entirely different level. But the difference between his success now compared to the past is that he is finally happy in his personal life, which he feels makes him a clearer thinker, greater creative problem solver, and more productive in his work life.

What we can learn from this is that if we surround ourselves with the right people in our personal lives, we can be freer and more successful in our professional lives because we have fewer personal distractions or baggage weighing us down.

SUMMARY: LIFE LESSONS FROM STEVEN HARVEY

- Don't allow imaginary obstacles to kill your dreams.
- Your dream must be important enough to conquer any hesitation in pursuing them.
- Start your destiny by discovering and embracing your gift.
- You will never be lifted up by tearing others down.
- The greatest personal and professional benefits come from investing in family.

"I'm in nobody's circle, I've always been an outsider."

—Joan Rivers

CHAPTER 45

JOAN RIVERS

Joan Rivers was a sharp-witted and iconoclastic comedian, television host, actress, writer, and Broadway star. Known for her big personality and superb fashion, Joan became the host of numerous red carpet events and shows that featured the best of what it meant to be a big star.

But in addition to her big personality, Joan also wrote 12 bestselling books, won a spoken word Grammy, launched her own jewelry line, and was the first woman to host a late night show in history *(The Late Show with Joan Rivers)*. She was ranked as one of the greatest—and funniest—comedians of all time, and was inducted into the Television Academy Hall of Fame before she passed away.

JOAN RIVERS' TOP 5 LIFE LESSONS

> "My audiences get younger all the time."

1. Recognize that there is a new generation behind you that you must inform and inspire.

   Joan was as "real" as real could be. And part of this realness was being open about all aspects of herself so that she could teach people about life.

   For example, Joan was open not only about her multiple plastic surgeries and her romantic life, but also about aging. She believed that it was better—and funnier—to discuss the absurdities of getting older rather than hiding them under the rug. And she believed it could get a good laugh too.

   The lesson that we can learn from this is that there is always a younger generation watching and observing us and if we are open about who we are—flaws and all—we can better serve them so they can be prepared for what's next in their lives, as we can be their examples and role models.

> "I have no methods; all I do is accept people as they are."

2. When you attempt to accept others—instead of trying to fix them—you will usher great peace into your life.

   Comedians are great observers of human beings—for better or for worse. And as an observer of other human beings, Joan got to see up close and personal the lives of super star celebrities like Johnny Carson, Prince Charles, and hundreds of others.

   From her experiences with them, for example, she concluded that people are people and you can't go around judging them for their flaws or trying to fix the things about them that you would like to change. This is one of the reasons why Joan became perhaps the most iconic red carpet host of all time because she accepted the quirkiness of those she was interacting with and took them at face value.

   But there was a flipside to this as well. Joan also accepted that some people just weren't very good—or nice or well-meaning—and she used their not so pleasant personalities and antics as material for her many comedy albums like *Rivers Presents Mr. Phyllis & Other Funny Stories*, among others. In other words, Joan believed that people—whether good or bad—should be accepted for who they are, not who we want them to be.

   What we can learn in our own lives is that instead of hoping or wishing people were something else, we should simply embrace who they are. And if who they are isn't helpful to us or making us a better person, we should accept this too and distance ourselves from them.

> "I succeeded by saying what everybody else is thinking."

3. Do not hide your deep-seated beliefs as when you speak them you will give permission to others to speak their thoughts too.

In addition to her standup and red carpet career, Joan starred in or created numerous television shows like *Celebrity Apprentice*, *Big Brother*, and *How'd You Get So Rich?* But these were only a handful of literally hundreds of appearances she made in entertainment because of her openness to speak her mind.

For example, Joan rose to fame after she became a guest on *The Tonight Show* with Johnny Carson as millions of people realized that she was vocalizing publicly what they were thinking or feeling privately. And Joan used this simple strategy to stay in the limelight for decades - by addressing things others were too afraid to speak about.

The takeaway here is that we often censor ourselves because we fear nobody will agree with or support us, but we really shouldn't. Joan's legendary career proves that there will always be other people who think like and support us, but we will never know it unless we speak up.

> "Life goes by fast. Enjoy it. Calm down. It's all funny. Next. Everyone gets so upset about the wrong things."

4. You must learn to slow your life down to the speed of enjoyment.

One of the things Joan was known for never doing was apologizing for her jokes. She believed people took things too seriously and as a result, she wanted to bring humor to even the most sensitive issues.

For example, she addressed celebrity weight gain, kidnappings, and numerous other touchy topics without fear of being bullied into censoring herself. And she did this because she felt the greatest medicine to help heal others was to make them laugh—even at inopportune moments.

What we can learn from this is that, with all of the darkness and tragedy in the world, if we don't learn to lighten up a bit we will never enjoy the time we have on the earth (however long or however brief).

> "I have become my own version of an optimist. If I can't make it through one door, I'll go through another door—or I'll make a door. Something terrific will come no matter how dark the present."

5. Only optimists can conquer the future.

Despite having acerbic humor, Joan really did believe that a positive mindset is the only thing that allowed her to succeed with so many diverse projects in arguably the most difficult industry in the world. From movies to television, to Broadway to comedy and beyond, Joan embraced the mantra that only optimists can conquer the future—and she was right.

SUMMARY: LIFE LESSONS FROM JOAN RIVERS

- The most important thing you can do is inspire the next generation.
- Usher greater peace into your life by accepting others rather than trying to fix them.
- Speaking your deepest beliefs gives others permission to do the same.
- Pace your life at the speed of enjoyment.
- Surrender your future to optimism.

"It never occurs to me that there are things I can't do."

—Whoopi Goldberg

CHAPTER 46
WHOOPI GOLDBERG

Whoopi Goldberg is an Emmy, Oscar, Grammy, and Tony award winning actor, television personality, and social activist. She had her first big breakthrough starring in *The Color Purple*, and went on to star in films like *Ghost, Sister Act, How Stella Got Her Groove Back, Girl, Interrupted*, and many others, making her the highest paid actress of all time at one point in her career.

But growing up, Whoopi was raised in the projects by a single mom. She dropped out of high school and had to work a variety of odd jobs to support herself, like being a bank teller, cosmologist, and bricklayer. Nevertheless, she followed her heart into acting and media and transformed herself into one of the greatest entertainment icons of all time.

WHOOPI GOLDBERG'S TOP 5 LIFE LESSONS

> "I am where I am because I believe in all possibilities."

1. Your beliefs can conquer your circumstances if you let them.

   As the daughter of a preacher and a nurse, Whoopi had a lot of structure, but very little money in her life. Nevertheless, she was still able to believe that she could transcend her circumstances and become more than what she was born into.

   For example, when she watched *Star Trek* on television as a little girl, she saw a Black female character (Uhura) and her life changed forever. From that point on, she believed that if somebody else who looked like her could be on television so could she.

   The lesson we can learn from this is that if somebody else has done what you want to do, it is possible that you can do it too. They might be a different person with different circumstances, but it means that it is possible for you to do what they've done. All you have to do is believe that achieving what they have is possible for you and then start working toward that achievement (step by simple step).

> "Art and life are subjective. Not everybody's gonna dig what I dig, but I reserve the right to dig it."

2. Never apologize for liking what you like.

As an artist and activist, Whoopi is used to being criticized by people over everything from how she looks, to the creative projects she takes on, to the social beliefs she espouses. But even with that criticism, she doesn't let it faze her because she understands that what she is drawn toward might be different than what others are drawn toward—and that's okay.

For example, even though Whoopi is one of the most awarded entertainers in history, she still has many haters, especially when she speaks openly on her show *The View*. Because she is decidedly liberal, there are those who dislike and distrust her simply because she has a different take on things than them. But instead of letting those who disagree with her get under her skin, she takes it as par for the course and moves on with her life.

For you and me, we can see from this example that no matter how successful we become, we will not be accepted by 100% of the people 100% of the time. Instead of letting this bother us, we should be grateful for the 50% or more of the people who do accept us and continue moving forward without worrying about the haters.

> "If you want to be somebody, if you want to go somewhere, you've got to wake up and pay attention."

3. Only those who observe how the world works are capable of succeeding in it.

Whoopi is an observational comedian, and she used her observations to develop a one-woman show in the 1980s in New York that caught the attention of a local director. Because the show was so good, the local director helped her get the show on Broadway where it caught the attention of Steven Spielberg, who became so smitten with Whoopi that he cast her in his film *The Color Purple*.

For Whoopi, it was her ability to observe the world and then speak openly—and jokingly—about it that allowed her to succeed beyond her wildest dreams. Without her watching how people and society works, she would have never had the kind of material she needed for the one woman show that eventually put her on the path to superstardom.

The takeaway here is that, whether in the performing arts, business, or other aspects of life, we should be constantly taking in the sights, sounds, and people around us so that we can better understand how the world works. Because the more we know how the world works, the better position we'll put ourselves in so that we can thrive within it.

> "If you don't look out for others, who will look out for you?"

4. You will always reap what you sow—so sow good things into others.

Few people know that Whoopi sits on several boards of directors dedicated to public service. For example, she is on the Board of Directors of the Jefferson Awards for Public Service, which recognizes local people who do extraordinary things outside of the limelight. And Whoopi sits on this board because she deeply believes that the world is truly a better place when people look out for each other (so she wants to look out for the people who are not calling attention to themselves).

What we can learn from this is that contrary to the popular belief that we should only look out for #1, looking out for others is what makes the world go round. If we did not have family, friends, coworkers, or even strangers who supported us on our own journeys, we wouldn't be anything in life.

> "It's being willing to walk away that gives you strength and power."

5. It has been said that the person who wants it least has the greatest leverage.

For many years, Whoopi was one of the most sought after actresses and comedians on the planet. She had her own late night talk show and starred in films as diverse as Made in *America* to *Muppets Tonight*. But then something happened.

Around the late 2000s, Whoopi's invitations to audition for and star in entertainment projects started to dry up. And they didn't dry up because she was less talented, more demanding, or did anything differently than what she was doing before; they dried up because sometimes there are dry seasons in life (even for legends). But instead of complaining about it, Whoopi simply decided to walk away from acting to show Hollywood how much they would miss her. And it worked.

Whoopi came roaring back to acting and starred in films ranging from *Toy Story 3* to *Teenage Mutant Ninja Turtles* and beyond, and proved to Tinseltown just how much they needed her.

The lesson here is that sometimes we have to walk away from something we love to show people just how valuable we are. When the right people feel our absence, they will want us to come back.

SUMMARY: LIFE LESSONS FROM WHOOPI GOLDBERG

- Circumstances can be conquered through powerful beliefs.
- Like what you like; never apologize.
- Succeed in the world by closely observing it.
- If you sow good things you will reap what you sow.
- You hold the greatest leverage when you care the least.

Appendix I: Quotes from Icons and Legends

Part I: Actors

Chapter 1: The Rock

- "One of the most important things you can accomplish is just being yourself."
- "All successes begin with self-discipline. It starts with you."
- "I've always loved the showmanship of professional wrestling. While I love making movies, I love that platform, too."
- "You either play the game or let the game play you."
- "If something stands between you and your success—move it. Never be denied."
- "It's you vs. you."

Chapter 2: Marilyn Monroe

- "Anything's possible, almost."
- "Success makes so many people hate you. I wish it wasn't that way. It would be wonderful to enjoy success without seeing envy in the eyes of those around you."
- "Fame doesn't fulfill you. It warms you a bit, but that warmth is temporary."
- "I don't stop when I'm tired. I only stop when I'm done."
- "Keep smiling, because life is a beautiful thing and there's so much to smile about."
- "If I'd observed all the rules I'd never have got anywhere."

Chapter 3: Clint Eastwood

- "I tried being reasonable, I didn't like it."
- "If a person doesn't change, there's something really wrong with him."

- "Fate pulls you in different directions."
- "I don't believe in pessimism."
- "I'm interested in the fact that the less secure a man is, the more likely he is to have extreme prejudice."
- "If I was not a dreamer, I would have achieved nothing."

Chapter 4: Leonardo DiCaprio

- "I want you to back yourself into a corner [and] give yourself no choice but to succeed."
- "I'm not the kind of person who tries to be cool or trendy, I'm definitely an individual."
- "Smile, nod, agree, and do whatever you were going to do anyway."
- "Pay close attention to the people who don't clap when you win."
- "Only you and you alone can change your situation. Don't blame it on anything or anyone."
- "To join the top 1% you have to do what the 99% won't."

Chapter 5: Angelina Jolie

- "Nothing would mean anything if I didn't live a life of use to others."
- "When I get logical…that's when I get in trouble."
- "I don't see the point of doing an interview unless you're going to share the things you learned and the mistakes you make. So, to admit that I'm extremely human and have done some dark things I don't think makes me unusual or unusually dark. I think it is actually the right thing to do, and I'd like to think it's the right thing to do."

- "Anytime I feel lost, I pull out a map and stare. I stare until I have reminded myself that life is a giant adventure, so much to do, to see."
- "We come to love not by finding the perfect person, but learning to see an imperfect person perfectly."
- "Jump forward, mean well, commit, and just see what happens."

Chapter 6: Marlon Brando

- "What might be a brave choice for you, for another person they may simply not experience fear."
- "If we are not our brother's keeper, at least let us not be his executioner."
- "We make up any excuse to preserve myths about people we love, but the reverse is also true; if we dislike an individual we adamantly resist changing our opinion, even when somebody offers proof of his decency, because it's vital to have myths about both the gods and devils in our lives."
- "We only have so many faces in our pockets."
- "Too much success can ruin you as surely as too much failure."
- "I refuse to be a fool dancing on a string held by all those big shots."

Chapter 7: George Clooney

- "Everybody needs a co-pilot."
- "You have only a short period of time in life to make your mark."
- "I had to stop going to auditions thinking, 'Oh, I hope they like me. I had to start thinking I was the answer to their problem."

- "When you're young you believe it when people tell you how good you are. And that's the danger, you inhale. Everyone will tell you you're a genius, which you're not, and if you understand that, you win."
- "It's not about an opening weekend. It's about a career, building a set of films you're proud of. Period."
- "Peace, like war, must be waged."

Chapter 8: Cary Grant

- "Destiny is not necessarily something we get out of life, but rather, what we give."
- "I pretended to be somebody I wanted to be until I finally became that person. Or he became me."
- "No greater honor can come to any man than the respect of his colleagues."
- "There's no point in being unhappy about growing older. Just think of the millions who have been denied that privilege."
- "It takes 500 small details to add up to one favorable impression."
- "Insanity runs in my family."

Chapter 9: Jennifer Lawrence

- "We need to tell each other our stories."
- "If something seems difficult or impossible, it interests me."
- "It's not until we get older that we realize that other people exist."
- "Don't worry about unkind people…because you come across people like that throughout your life."
- "Things can happen to you but they don't have to happen to your soul."

- "Everything has beauty but not everybody can see it."

Chapter 10: Keanu Reeves

- "Sometimes we get so caught up in our day to day lives that we forget to take time out to enjoy the beauty in life."
- "If you can make a woman laugh, you're seeing the most beautiful thing on God's earth."
- "The simple act of paying attention can take you a long way."
- "When you truly understand karma, then you realize you are responsible for everything in your life. It is incredibly empowering to know that your future is in your hands."
- "If you have been brutally broken but still have the courage to be gentle to other living things, then you're a bad*ss with a heart of an angel."
- "Sometimes enemies are our best teachers."

Chapter 11: Sylvester Stallone

- "Every champion was once a contender that refused to give up."
- "Consider the source. Don't be a fool by listening to a fool."
- "I have great expectations for the future because the past was highly overrated."
- "Once in one's life, for one mortal moment, one must make a grab for immortality; if not, one has not lived."
- "I stopped thinking the way other people think a long time ago. You gotta think like you think."
- "I believe any success in life is made by going into an area with blind and furious optimism."

Chapter 12: Lady Gaga

- "You have to be the antithesis of the status quo. You have to work against it."
- "If you don't have any shadows, you're not in the light."
- "I want people to walk around delusional about how great they can be—and then fight so hard for it every day that the lie becomes the truth."
- "Brushes with darkness won't help you create your destiny."
- "Celebrate the things you don't like about yourself."
- "I don't want to be a celebrity, I want to make a difference."

Chapter 13: John Wayne

- "You're short on ears and long on mouth."
- "Courage is being afraid and going on the journey anyhow."
- "When you stop fighting, that's death."
- "I'm responsible only for what I say, not for what you understand."
- "I have tried to live life so that my family would love me and my friends respect me."
- "Tomorrow hopes we have learned something from yesterday."

Chapter 14: Hugh Jackman

- "Respect motivates me, not success."
- "If you back down from the fear, the ghost of that fear never goes away."
- "Anyone who thinks they're indispensable is fooling themselves."
- "I'd sell my soul for a good cause."
- "Your religion should be in your actions."

Chapter 15: Denzel Washington

- "You have to grab moments when they happen."
- "You pray for rain, you gotta deal with the mud too. That's part of it."
- "The chances you take, the people you meet, the people you love, the faith you have. That's what's going to define you."
- "To me, success is inner peace."
- "Man gives you the award but God gives you the reward."
- "My ultimate life dream project is my kids. My family."

Chapter 16: Viola Davis

- "When you see what the deficit is, then you have to do something about it."
- "When you pray, God puts people in your life to lead you where you cannot lead yourself."
- "Even when I get the fried chicken special, I have to dig into it like it's filet mignon."
- "The privilege of a lifetime is being who you are."
- "Artists can only be truth tellers."
- "I don't have time to stay up all night worrying about what someone who doesn't love me has to say about me."

Chapter 17: Heath Ledger

- "I'm in control of my life, not anyone in Hollywood."
- "I feel like I'm wasting time if I repeat myself."
- "If you are just safe about the choices you make, you won't grow."
- "I completely live in the now, not in the past, not in the future."
- "Never give up on what makes you smile."

- "As long as you have a clear picture of the life you want to lead, eventually you'll get there."

Chapter 18: Humphrey Bogart

- "You're not a star until they can spell your name in Karachi."
- "I always cry at weddings, especially my own."
- "Everybody has something to conceal."
- "There is more to talking than just words."
- "The way to survive an Oscar is never to try to win another one."
- "A hotdog at the game beats roast beef at the Ritz."

Chapter 19: Queen Latifah

- "I'm a strong person with or without this person, with or without this job, and with or without these tight pants."
- "Life is much bigger, grander, higher, and wider than we allow ourselves to think. We're capable of so much more than we allow ourselves to believe."
- "Most people don't have so much talent that they can become a success all their own. We all need people to help us and lift us up."
- "When I was around 18, I looked in the mirror and said, 'You're either going to love yourself or hate yourself.' And I decided to love myself. That changed a lot of things."
- "I decided early on that I was going to put on my crown and rule my world by acting right and treating myself like a queen."
- "How many crossroads are you allowed to have in life? I seem to have a lot of crossroads. I think maybe I crossed back across the same road too often."

Chapter 20: Arnold Schwarzenegger

- "Do not bring me small ideas; bring me big ideas."
- "The worst thing I can be is the same as everybody else. I hate that."
- "Being surrounded by winners helps you develop into a winner."
- "Don't go where it's crowded. Go where it's empty. Even though it's harder to get there, that's where you belong and that's where there's less competition."
- "You have to remember something: everybody pities the weak. Jealousy has to be earned."
- "You'll get more from being a peacemaker than a warrior."

Chapter 21: Sidney Poitier

- "I am the me I chose to be."
- "I had chosen to use my work as a reflection of my values."
- "I have always been a learner because I knew nothing."
- "I've learned that I have to find positive outlets for anger or it will destroy me."
- "If I'm remembered for having done a few good things, and if my presence here has sparked some good energies, that's plenty."
- "The only weapon I had was to say no."

Chapter 22: Anthony Hopkins

- "In certain moment's in our lives we get little signals, little flashes that say it's yours if you want it."
- "Once you begin to fall off the track and believe you breathe different air to everyone else, you're doomed; you're finished."

- "Beware of the tyranny of the weak. They just suck you dry."
- "Today is the tomorrow I was worried about yesterday."
- "I would hope not to be so arrogant as to doubt anybody's religion or belief."
- "Life's too short to deal with other people's insecurities."

Chapter 23: Katharine Hepburn

- "Love has nothing to do with what you are expecting to get, only with what you are expecting to give."
- "If you obey all the rules you miss all the fun."
- "It would be a terrific innovation if you could get your mind to stretch a little further than the next wisecrack."
- "I don't care what is written about me so long as it isn't true."
- "The time to make up your mind about people is never."
- "Life is full of censorship."

Chapter 24: Michael Keaton

- "No, I don't see many movies. I don't even see my own movies."
- "Dying is a really hard way to learn about life."
- "There comes a point in your life when you realize how quickly time goes by, and how quickly it has gone. Then it really speeds up exponentially."
- "I never saw what I do for a living as who I am."
- "I'm just shocked at how blatantly shallow people are sometimes."
- "I choose not to be at the whim of others. I want to be at my own whim."

Chapter 25: Michelle Pfeiffer...

- "Just standing around looking beautiful is so boring."
- "You have no idea what it's like to be famous until you become famous."
- "I don't know if it's naivete or narcissism, but I start out with this notion that I can do anything. It's not until I get into it that I realize what I've thrown myself into, and then I will do anything not to humiliate myself. And that, I think, is the secret to my success."
- "The anticipation of something is always much worse than the reality."
- "Love humiliates you."
- "The less you focus on your flaws, the better off you are."

Chapter 26: James Dean

- "Dream as if you'll live forever. Live as if you'll die today."
- "Only the gentle are ever really strong."
- "The gratification comes in the doing, not in the results."
- "Am I in love? Absolutely. I'm in love with ancient philosophers, foreign painters, classic authors, and musicians who have died long ago."
- "I think the prime reason for existence, for living in this world is discovery."
- "Remember: life is short, break the rules."

Part II: Comedians

Chapter 27: Kevin Hart

- "You only get one life. I'm going to embrace mine."

- "Everybody that is successful lays a blueprint out."
- "The day you stop doing the small things is the day you think you're above everybody else."
- "I don't care how busy I am, I will always make time for what is most important to me."
- "Whatever you've done, good or bad, it's nothing but preparation for the big events to come."
- "You can do the same thing with $20 million that you can do with $50 million. So, at a certain point in your life and in your career, you realize it's not about money."

Chapter 28: Conan O'Brien

- "If you work really hard, and you're kind, amazing things will happen."
- "Is it possible for a grown man to be body shamed by his own mirror?"
- "Every generation just wants their kids to have a better Spiderman reboot than they did."
- "All I ask is one thing, and I'm asking particularly of young people: please don't be cynical. I hate cynicism, for the record, it's my least favorite quality and it doesn't lead anywhere."
- "There are few things in this life more liberating than having your worst fear realized."
- "Remember that the story is never over."

Chapter 29: Jon Stewart

- I always knew I shouldn't have said that."
- "If you don't stick to your values when they're being tested, they're not values: they're hobbies."

- "If we amplify everything, we hear nothing."
- "I have complete faith in the continued absurdity of whatever's going on."
- "I'm not going to censor myself to comfort your ignorance."
- "The more you delve into science, the more it appears to rely on faith."

Chapter 30: Lucy Ball

- "I'm not funny. What I am is brave."
- "Love yourself first and everything else falls into line. You really have to love yourself to get anything done in this world."
- "I think knowing what you cannot do is more important than knowing what you can."
- "Don't let the brightness of the big goal blind you to what happens on the way toward the goal."
- "One of the things I learned the hard way was that it doesn't pay to get discouraged. Keeping busy and making optimism a way of life can restore faith in yourself."
- "Not everything that is faced can be changed, but nothing can be changed until it is faced."

Chapter 31: Charlie Chaplain

- "To be able to truly laugh you must be able to take your pain and play with it!"
- "Our knowledge has made us cynical. Our cleverness, hard and unkind. We think too much and feel too little. More than machinery we need humanity. More than cleverness we need kindness and gentleness. Without these qualities, life will be violent and all will be lost..."

- "That's the trouble with the world. We all despise ourselves."
- "Life can be wonderful if you're not afraid of it."
- "Nothing is permanent in this wicked world—not even our troubles."
- "You'll never find a rainbow if you're looking down."

Chapter 32: Danny DeVito

- "A tree falls the way it leans. Be careful the way you lean."
- "The whole point of love is to put someone else's needs above your own."
- "You have to give people permission to laugh."
- "I think you do your best work when you take chances, when you're not safe, when you're not in the middle of the road."
- "A bad salesman will automatically drop his price. Bad salesmen make me sick."
- "There are two dilemmas that rattle the human mind: how do you hang onto someone who won't stay? And how do you get rid of someone who won't go?"

Part III: Directors & Studio Magnets

Chapter 33: Steven Spielberg

- "When I grow up, I still want to be a director."
- "All of us every single year, we're a different person. I don't think we're the same person all our lives."
- "All of my movies are about how I wish the world would work."
- "I don't dream at night, I dream at day, I dream all day."
- "The delicate balance of mentoring someone is not creating them in your own image, but giving them the opportunity to create themselves."

- "Even though I get older, what I do never gets old, and that's what I think keeps me hungry."

Chapter 34: George Lucas

- "We are all living in cages with the door wide open."
- "You don't always know exactly what you're doing and you shouldn't."
- "If you're really doing something worthwhile, I think you will be pushed to the brink of hopelessness before you come through to the other side."
- "Someday you're going to have to separate what seems to be important from what really is important."
- "My success wasn't based on how I could push down everybody that was around me. My success was based on how much I could push everybody up."
- "All the skill in the world isn't going to help you unless you have something to say."

Chapter 35: Spike Lee

- "I think people who have faults are a lot more interesting than people who are perfect."
- "I think it's very important that films make people look at what they've forgotten."
- "I'm not going to let other people dictate to me who I should be or the stories I should tell."
- "It gets dangerous when you start allowing people to validate your work."
- "A lot of times we censor ourselves before the censor even gets there."

- "It's been my observation that parents kill more dreams than anybody."

Chapter 36: James Cameron

- "Curiosity is the most powerful thing you own."
- "Don't put limitations on yourself. Others will do that for you."
- "Your only competitors are your past achievements."
- "The future is not set. There is no fate but what we make."
- "If you set your goals ridiculously high and it's a failure, you will fail above everyone else's success."
- "You have to not listen to the naysayers because there will be many and often they'll be much more qualified than you and cause you to sort of doubt yourself."

Chapter 37: Quentin Tarantino

- "Just because you are a character doesn't mean you have character."
- "I want to top expectations. I want to blow you away."
- "I don't believe in elitism. I don't think the audience is this dumb person lower than me. I am the audience."
- "Emotion will always win over coolness and cleverness."
- "It's my job to look at other people's humanity."
- "Personality goes a long way."

Chapter 38: Walt Disney

- "First, think. Second, believe. Third, dream. And finally, dare."
- "Imagination has no age. Dreams are forever."
- "All you've got to do is own up to your ignorance honestly,

- and you'll find people who are eager to fill your head with information."
- "That's the trouble with the world, too many people grow up. They forget."
- "We keep moving forward, opening new doors, and doing new things, because we're curious and curiosity keeps leading us down new paths."
- "We are not trying to entertain the critics. I'll take my chances with the public."

Chapter 39: Stan Lee

- "It's fun doing something that hasn't been done before."
- "I don't have inspiration. I only have ideas. Ideas and deadlines."
- "I don't really see a need to retire as long as I'm having fun."
- "Every day is a new adventure."
- "I used to be embarrassed because I was just a comic book writer while other people were building bridges or going on to medical careers. And then I began to realize: entertainment is one of the most important things in people's lives. Without it, they might go off on the deep end."
- "No one has a perfect life. Everyone has something that he wishes was not the way it is."

Part IV: Talk Show Hosts

Chapter 40: Oprah

- "The great courageous act that we must all do is have the courage to step out of our history and past so we can live our dreams."
- "Turn your wounds into wisdom."

- "Every time you suppress some part of yourself or allow others to play you small, you are ignoring the owner's manual your Creator gave you."
- "Everyone is keeper of a dream."
- "You don't become what you want, you become what you believe."
- "When I look to the future it is so bright it burns my eyes!"

Chapter 41: Barbara Walters

- "A man cannot be made to feel uncomfortable without his own approval."
- "Fight the big fight, don't fight the little fight."
- "A big laugh makes any interview, any conversation, so much better."
- "The hardest thing you will ever do is trust yourself."
- "Personal gain is empty if you do not feel you have positively touched another's life."
- "Success can go one of two ways. It can make you a prima donna—or it can smooth the edges, take away the insecurities, let the nice things come out."

Chapter 42: Larry King

- "I never learned anything while I was talking."
- "If you do something, expect consequences."
- "You cannot talk to people successfully if you are not interested in what they have to say or you have no respect for them."
- "Getting your house in order and reducing the confusion gives you more control over your life. Personal organization

somehow releases or frees you to operate more effectively."
- "There is nothing in your destiny, nothing in your future that you cannot accomplish."
- "Even those who have a natural ability for something have to work to develop it."

Chapter 43: Tyra Banks

- "Never dull your shine for somebody else."
- "Perfect is boring, human is beautiful"
- "I became the victim of myself."
- "You've got to learn to accept the fool in you, as well as the part that's got it goin' on."
- "There's always going to be dreams and goals I have, but I never really tell people what they are."
- "There's no excuse for rudeness."

Chapter 44: Steve Harvey

- "Your career is what you're paid for. Your calling is what you're made for."
- "Don't let your mind stop you."
- "Your dream has to be bigger than your fear."
- "Your mission, your purpose, and your destiny will all be tied to one thing - your gift."
- "Stop wasting time looking at somebody else's reality while doing nothing about yours."
- "When you're happy at home, you can make a lot of things happen."

Chapter 45: Joan Rivers

- "I'm in nobody's circle, I've always been an outsider."
- "My audiences get younger all the time."
- "I have no methods; all I do is accept people as they are."
- "I succeeded by saying what everybody else is thinking."
- "Life goes by fast. Enjoy it. Calm down. It's all funny. Next. Everyone gets so upset about the wrong things."
- "I have become my own version of an optimist. If I can't make it through one door, I'll go through another door—or I'll make a door. Something terrific will come no matter how dark the present."

Chapter 46: Whoopi Goldberg

- "It never occurs to me that there are things I can't do."
- "I am where I am because I believe in all possibilities."
- "Art and life are subjective. Not everybody's gonna dig what I dig, but I reserve the right to dig it."
- "If you want to be somebody, if you want to go somewhere, you've got to wake up and pay attention."
- "If you don't look out for others, who will look out for you?"
- "It's being willing to walk away that gives you strength and power."

Appendix II: Life Lessons from Icons and Legends

Part I: Actors

Chapter 1: The Rock

1. Success can only be achieved through systematically disciplining yourself.
2. The most successful people always put on the best shows.
3. In the game of life, you must understand its invisible rules to win.
4. In the face of obstacles, focus and tenacity will make you unstoppable.
5. Double down on your goals AFTER you have reached your greatness.

Chapter 2: Marilyn Monroe

1. The downside of achievement is the haters it breeds.
2. If you only pursue things to be recognized, you will never be satisfied when you get them.
3. Fatigue should not be an excuse to give up.
4. When you slow the world down, you can see more of the beauty in it.
5. Break out of the prison others have tried to lock you up in.

Chapter 3: Clint Eastwood

1. If you're still the same person you used to be, you have missed out on most of life.
2. Life is a puzzle, not a recipe.
3. Cynics never change the world.
4. Insecure people are often the most judgmental.

5. Only dreamers can change their world—and change the world.

Chapter 4: Leonardo DiCaprio

   1. Real winners stay true to themselves.
   2. You don't need anyone else's permission to win.
   3. Always know who is for you.
   4. Once you refuse to be a victim, life becomes limitless.
   5. Almost everyone knows the formula to success but almost nobody uses it.

Chapter 5: Angelina Jolie

   1. Sometimes trying to "figure things out" is the worst thing you can do.
   2. Only open your mouth to teach, inspire, or empower.
   3. The world is much bigger than "your world," so go out and explore it.
   4. True love is not based on perfection, but on perspective.
   5. Failure only happens when you refuse to leave your house.

Chapter 6: Marlon Brando

   1. The lack of empathy is one of the greatest threats to our lives—and to humanity.
   2. People only believe the story about your life they want to believe.
   3. You must decide whether you will wear your real face or somebody else's.
   4. Gaining the world can leave you in the same place as losing it.

5. To achieve greatness, cut the strings of those trying to control you.

Chapter 7: George Clooney

1. Your greatest successes will often come during short seasons of intense productivity.
2. Never think of yourself as a grasshopper, think of yourself as a giant.
3. Smoke but don't inhale.
4. Your life is an entire book, not just a single chapter.
5. Being intentional about every aspect of your life will create positive results.

Chapter 8: Cary Grant

1. Practice who you want to become.
2. Be a pleasant experience for those around you.
3. Embrace all of the miles you have traveled.
4. It's the small things that make all of the difference.
5. Your family isn't the only one that is crazy.

Chapter 9: Jennifer Lawrence

1. To achieve on the highest levels, you have to think on the highest levels.
2. Wisdom begins when we see the world from somebody else's perspective.
3. Jerks come and go, but we don't have to get bent out of shape by them.
4. Resilience occurs when you refuse to let pain stay in your soul.

5. If we look long enough, we can see how truly special the people and things are around us.

Chapter 10: Keanu Reeves

1. Laughter is medicine every human heart needs.
2. The greater your focus the greater your future.
3. You are the solution you have been looking for all of your life.
4. You can still live life as an angel even if you have been to hell and back.
5. Our opponents often teach us greater lessons than our friends do.

Chapter 11: Sylvester Stallone

1. Your success or failure depends on the people you choose to believe.
2. If your past looks brighter than your future, start working toward building yourself a bigger masterpiece.
3. Sometimes you have to put all of your eggs in one basket even if you can't guarantee the outcome.
4. Success comes from breaking away from the crowd, not following it.
5. Energy and optimism are two of the most overlooked aspects of success.

Chapter 12: Lady Gaga

1. Recognizing there are things you must change about yourself is the first step to living peacefully with others.
2. The positive thoughts you think about yourself can override

your negative or average circumstances if only you'll apply what you believe.
3. Playing with fire burns the bridges you need for your future.
4. Using reverse psychology will help you see that your perceived flaws aren't really flaws at all.
5. Only you can decide if your life will be about success or significance.

Chapter 13: John Wayne

1. Even if the odds don't look good, roll the dice anyway.
2. Quitting isn't failure, it's surrender.
3. You never have to explain yourself to those unwilling to "hear" you.
4. Being a hero to those who know you best is the sign of a life well lived.
5. Your future doesn't need to be a blank canvass.

Chapter 14: Hugh Jackman

1. Quitting defeats more people than losing does.
2. There is only one master of the universe and it is not you or me.
3. One of the greatest rewards in life is investing all of yourself to improve other people's lives.
4. Thinking we are "good people" is not enough; we actually must become the best version of ourselves.

Chapter 15: Denzel Washington

1. Every dream you have will at times require you to walk

through a nightmare.
2. The people who get the most out of life are the ones who embrace all of its unexpected surprises.
3. A heart full of joy is better than a bank account full of money.
4. The blessings you receive now are nothing compared to the blessings that are to come.
5. We reproduce what we are, not who we think we are.

Chapter 16: Viola Davis

1. Your journey to greatness is meant to be taken with others.
2. Treat everything you do with class.
3. The greatest reward you can ever receive is recognizing how special you truly are.
4. The world needs you to tell the truth about it.
5. Never meditate on the criticisms of your haters.

Chapter 17: Heath Ledger

1. Life only gets interesting if you try new things.
2. Rewards only flow to individuals who reach for them.
3. Being present eliminates the distractions of tomorrow and yesterday.
4. If you settle for average, your soul will never leap with joy.
5. Once you decide on a destination, your mind figures out a roadmap to get there.

Chapter 18: Humphrey Bogart

1. It's okay to laugh at yourself.
2. Nobody is as they appear.

3. You must master how to talk with your body.
4. Life is about more than trophies and awards.
5. Even movie stars never outgrow the simple pleasures of life.

Chapter 19: Queen Latifah

1. Magic exists if only you will search for it.
2. Your success depends not only on your hard work, but on other people helping you along the way.
3. The number 1 secret to self-care is liking and respecting the person staring back at you in the mirror.
4. Becoming the best version of yourself begins by acting like the best version of yourself.
5. The quality of your life depends on the choices you make over and over again.

Chapter 20: Arnold Schwarzenegger

1. If two people are the same, one of them is unnecessary—don't let it be you.
2. Success can be predicted by who you hang out with.
3. Pick a narrow niche and become the best in the world at it.
4. If you have no haters, you haven't reached the peak of your greatness yet.
5. The most successful people on earth know how to get along with others.

Chapter 21: Sidney Poitier

1. Never divorce what you do from who you are.
2. Accepting that you need to learn more than you currently do

is the first step in becoming greater.
3. Your emotions are only helpful when you can channel them toward something constructive.
4. True success only comes down to a few simple things.
5. Your "no" can be the best choice you ever make.

Chapter 22: Anthony Hopkins

1. Arrogance will bury you.
2. The bigger you become, the more others will think you owe them something.
3. Living too much in the past or future brings unnecessary anxiety.
4. Respecting others' beliefs is not the same as agreeing with them.
5. Do not spend time with people who have no control over themselves.

Chapter 23: Katharine Hepburn

1. Only those that challenge the status quo are remembered by history.
2. The most intelligent minds cultivate a long-term perspective.
3. Your personal privacy is nobody else's business.
4. Very little is accomplished when you jump to conclusions about others.
5. History is rarely made by those who censor themselves or play it safe.

Chapter 24: Michael Keaton

1. Begin regularly reflecting on life lessons to reduce the number of future regrets.
2. You may only have 30,000-40,000 days on the earth, so use them wisely.
3. Your work, success, and accomplishments are not your identity.
4. Most people won't ever try to know the real you.
5. If you don't decide what your schedule will be, others will.

Chapter 25: Michelle Pfeiffer

1. Imagining something is different than experiencing it.
2. Success begins when you start, not when you achieve.
3. The worst part about fear is thinking about it, no living through it.
4. When you truly love something—or someone—you must fully surrender your ego to it.
5. Never meditate on what makes you weak, meditate on what makes you strong.

Chapter 26: James Dean

1. The strongest people in the world are the most loving.
2. True meaning and success is found in the pursuit of your dream, not just the attainment of it.
3. Look to the greatest figures of the past to accelerate your progress in the present.
4. If there was nothing new to see or experience in life, what is the point?
5. You have no time to fit in the square box others are trying to force you into.

Part II: Comedians

Chapter 27: Kevin Hart

1. You must write out the vision you have for your life and how you will get it.
2. The small things are always more important than people realize.
3. Continuously prioritizing what is important is one of the most difficult things you will ever do.
4. Your entire life is a test.
5. One day you will realize that enough is truly enough.

Chapter 28: Conan O'Brien

1. Humility is one the most overlooked qualities in success.
2. Building a better future for the next generation is critically important.
3. Dreams are not buried in failure, they're buried in doubt.
4. Overcoming your nightmares make you unstoppable.
5. You will never stop being a work-in-progress.

Chapter 29: Jon Stewart

1. Icons hold onto their beliefs even when they're not convenient.
2. Become quiet enough to recognize the difference between the important and the trivial.
3. Learn to develop a sense of perspective about the wackiness of life.
4. You possess information others do not, so do not be afraid to educate them about it.
5. The greatest minds realize they don't know much of anything.

Chapter 30: Lucy Ball

1. The world doesn't need to accept you, you need to accept you.
2. Building your life on your strengths and not your weaknesses will multiply your success.
3. Happiness is found in the journey, not the destination.
4. Assassinate all discouragement in your life if you want to achieve great things.
5. Running toward your problems—not away from them—is the only way you can get the victory you deserve.

Chapter 31: Charlie Chaplain

1. A head full of knowledge must always be matched by a heart full of love.
2. Self-hatred is more common than self-love.
3. Victory goes to the bold, not the cautious.
4. The only thing that will never change is that things will always change.
5. To elevate to the higher you cannot stay focused on the lower.

Chapter 32: Danny DeVito

1. True love abandons selfishness.
2. Always give people the room to be themselves.
3. Greatness happens when you become the most extreme version of yourself.
4. If you have something valuable, don't give it away for nothing.
5. Curating the right circle will be one of the greatest challenges of your life.

Part III: Directors & Studio Wizards

Chapter 33: Steven Spielberg

1. We have to be willing to become new—and better—versions of ourselves over and over again.
2. Never accept the status quo, improve it.
3. It is possible to live your dreams everyday if you simply decide to.
4. The greatest gift you can give to another is helping them become who they are called to be.
5. Choose a career interesting enough to keep you excited all of your life.

Chapter 34: George Lucas

1. Be open to making unexpected detours on your journey to success.
2. The bigger your goal, the bigger your battle.
3. Greatness lies in recognizing the difference between what is kinda cool from what is absolutely necessary.
4. There is no higher calling of a leader than to make others better.
5. Take time to develop your unique and original voice.

Chapter 35: Spike Lee

1. Remembering the best - and worst - of the past will help you become a better decision maker and an all-around better person.
2. If you never decide who you want to be, somebody else will try to do it for you.

3. There will always be somebody who adores what you do - and somebody who absolutely abhors it too.
4. You are not called to stay quiet and blend in; you are called to be loud and stand out.
5. Sometimes those closest to you will misunderstand why you were put on this earth.

Chapter 36: James Cameron

1. Others can only stop you if you let them.
2. Always believe your greatest days are ahead of you, not behind you.
3. You can create any future you want through meticulous decision making.
4. The only way you can be a player in the big leagues is if you aim to be.
5. Even most successful people won't recognize your potential until you have achieved it.

Chapter 37: Quentin Tarantino

1. Always give people a "wow factor."
2. Greatness manifests when you recognize that you are neither superior or inferior to others.
3. People will reward you for a lifetime if you can take them on an emotional journey.
4. Never forget that all of the faces in the crowd are more than just anonymous statistics.
5. Showing your uniqueness carries greater rewards than you think.

Chapter 38: Walt Disney...

1. You will never outgrow your dreams.
2. The more humble you are about your own limitations, the more others will want to help you.
3. When life becomes about chores and not fun, it's too late.
4. Curiosity is the first step toward changing the world—or, at least, changing your world.
5. Do not live your life for the haters—they will hate you no matter what.

Chapter 39: Stan Lee

1. To become great, you do not need to wait for inspiration to get started.
2. Do not create a life you want to retire from.
3. You can find magic when you look for it.
4. Always remember no matter what you do, it is just as important as what others are doing too.
5. Perfection only exists in fairy tales.

Part IV: Talk Show Hosts

Chapter 40: Oprah

1. No matter who you are, life will present you with one all-defining choice: to become bitter OR become better as a result of the wounds other people and circumstances have caused you.
2. You don't have to live in the boxes other people try to force you in.
3. God gives you a dream that only you are qualified to bring

into existence.
  4. Your beliefs are powerful enough to rearrange your circumstances.
  5. If you chase the future you will eventually catch it.

Chapter 41: Barbara Walters

1. The size of your battles determines the size of your rewards.
2. Loosening up a bit will multiply your friendships.
3. Believing in yourself starts with accepting that you are not an accident.
4. No real success means anything unless you have lifted up others along the way.
5. Success, more than failure, will reveal who you are underneath.

Chapter 42: Larry King

1. When you do things that winners do, you will win.
2. The best conversationalists are truly curious about what others are telling them.
3. A successful life is usually an organized one.
4. Achieving something - small or great - starts with believing that you can.
5. Turning your natural talent into skill through discipline is the quickest path to greatness.

Chapter 43: Tyra Banks

1. To become an icon, realness must be valued over perfection.
2. Your own negative thoughts and behaviors can harm you more than you realize.

3. Every person has an Aristotle and Homer Simpson inside of them.
   4. People need to earn the right to know the plans you have for your future.
   5. No matter how important, successful, busy, distracted, angry, or hurt you are, if you prioritize being kind to others you will always be a winner in life.

Chapter 44: Steve Harvey

   1. Imaginary obstacles kill more dreams than real ones do.
   2. If your dream is important enough, it will override any hesitation in pursuing it.
   3. The minute you discover and embrace your gift is the minute your destiny begins.
   4. Tearing others down will never lift you up.
   5. Strongly investing in your family life will not only bring personal benefits, but also professional benefits too.

Chapter 45: Joan Rivers

   1. Recognize that there is a new generation behind you that you must inform and inspire.
   2. When you attempt to accept others—instead of trying to fix them—you will usher great peace into your life.
   3. Do not hide your deep-seated beliefs as when you speak them you will give permission to others to speak their thoughts too.
   4. You must learn to slow your life down to the speed of enjoyment.
   5. Only optimists can conquer the future.

Chapter 46: Whoopi Goldberg

1. Your beliefs can conquer your circumstances if you let them.
2. Never apologize for liking what you like.
3. Only those who observe how the world works are capable of succeeding in it.
4. You will always reap what you sow—so sow good things into others.
5. It has been said that the person who wants it least has the greatest leverage.

WORKS CITED

Chapter 1

1. Dwayne Johnson quotes. 2022. Accessed from: https://www.brainyquote.com/authors/dwayne-johnson-quotes
2. Dwayne Johnson biography. 2022. Accessed from: https://www.biography.com/actor/dwayne-johnson

Chapter 2

3. Marilyn Monroe quotes. 2022. Accessed from: https://www.brainyquote.com/authors/marilyn-monroe-quotes
4. Marilyn Monroe biography. 2022. Accessed from: https://www.biography.com/actor/marilyn-monroe

Chapter 3

5. Clint Eastwood quotes. 2022. Accessed from: https://www.brainyquote.com/authors/clint-eastwood-quotes
6. Clint Eastwood biography. 2022. Accessed from: https://www.biography.com/actor/clint-eastwood

Chapter 4

7. Leonardo DiCaprio quotes. 2022. Accessed from: https://www.brainyquote.com/authors/leonardo-dicaprio-quotes
8. Leonardo DiCaprio biography. 2022. Accessed from: https://www.biography.com/actor/leonardo-dicaprio

Chapter 5

9. Angelina Jolie quotes. 2022. Accessed from: https://www.

brainyquote.com/authors/angelina-jolie-quotes
10. Angelina Jolie biography. 2022. Accessed from: https://www.biography.com/actor/angelina-jolie

Chapter 6

11. Marlon Brando quotes. 2022. Accessed from: https://www.brainyquote.com/authors/marlon-brando-quotes
12. Marlon Brando biography. 2022. Accessed from: https://www.biography.com/actor/marlon-brando

Chapter 7

13. George Clooney quotes. 2022. Accessed from: https://www.brainyquote.com/authors/george-clooney-quotes
14. George Clooney biography. 2022. Accessed from: https://www.biography.com/actor/george-clooney

Chapter 8

15. Cary Grant quotes. 2022. Accessed from: https://www.brainyquote.com/authors/cary-grant-quotes
16. Cary Grant biography. 2022. Accessed from: https://www.biography.com/actor/cary-grant

Chapter 9

17. Jennifer Lawrence quotes. 2022. Accessed from: https://www.brainyquote.com/authors/jennifer-lawrence-quotes
18. Jennifer Lawrence biography. 2022. Accessed from: https://www.biography.com/actor/jennifer-lawrence

Chapter 10

19. Keanu Reeves quotes. 2022. Accessed from: https://www.brainyquote.com/authors/keanu-reeves-quotes
20. Keanu Reeves biography. 2022. Accessed from: https://www.biography.com/actor/keanu-reeves

Chapter 11

21. Sylvester Stalone quotes. 2022. Accessed from: https://www.brainyquote.com/authors/sylvester-stallone-quotes
22. Sylvester Stalone biography. 2022. Accessed from: https://www.biography.com/actor/sylvester-stallone

Chapter 12

23. Lady Gaga quotes. 2022. Accessed from: https://www.brainyquote.com/authors/lady-gaga-quotes
24. Lady Gaga biography. 2022. Accessed from: https://www.biography.com/musician/lady-gaga

Chapter 13

25. John Wayne quotes. 2022. Accessed from: https://www.brainyquote.com/authors/john-wayne-quotes
26. John Wayne biography. 2022. Accessed from: https://www.biography.com/actor/john-wayne

Chapter 14

27. Hugh Jackman quotes. 2022. Accessed from: https://www.brainyquote.com/authors/hugh-jackman-quotes

28. Hugh Jackman biography. 2022. Accessed from: https://www.biography.com/actor/hugh-jackman

Chapter 15

29. Denzel Washington quotes. 2022. Accessed from: https://www.brainyquote.com/authors/denzel-washington-quotes
30. Denzel Washington biography. 2022. Accessed from: https://www.biography.com/actor/denzel-washington

Chapter 16

31. Viola Davis quotes. 2022. Accessed from: https://www.brainyquote.com/authors/viola-davis-quotes
32. Viola Davis Biography. 2022. Accessed from: https://www.biography.com/actor/viola-davis

Chapter 17

33. Heath Ledger quotes. 2022. Accessed from: https://www.brainyquote.com/authors/heath-ledger-quotes
34. Heath Ledger biography. 2022. Accessed from: https://www.biography.com/actor/heath-ledger

Chapter 18

35. Humphrey Bogart quotes. 2022. Accessed from: https://www.brainyquote.com/authors/humphrey-bogart-quotes
36. Humphrey Bogart biography. 2022. Accessed from: https://www.biography.com/actor/humphrey-bogart

Chapter 19

37. Queen Latifah quotes. 2022. Accessed from: https://www.brainyquote.com/authors/queen-latifah-quotes
38. Queen Latifah biography. 2022. Accessed from: https://www.biography.com/musician/queen-latifah

Chapter 20

39. Arnold Schwarzenegger quotes. 2022. Accessed from: https://www.brainyquote.com/authors/arnold-schwarzenegger-quotes
40. Arnold Schwarzenegger biography. 2022. Accessed from: https://www.biography.com/actor/arnold-schwarzenegger

Chapter 21

41. Sidney Poitier quotes. 2022. Accessed from: https://www.brainyquote.com/authors/sidney-poitier-quotes
42. Sidney Poitier biography. 2022. Accessed from: https://www.biography.com/actor/sidney-poitier

Chapter 22

43. Anthony Hopkins quotes. 2022. Accessed from: https://www.brainyquote.com/authors/anthony-hopkins-quotes
44. Anthony Hopkins biography. 2022. Accessed from: https://www.biography.com/actor/anthony-hopkins

Chapter 23

45. Katharine Hepburn quotes. 2022. Accessed from: https://www.brainyquote.com/authors/katharine-hepburn-quotes
46. Katharine Hepburn biography. 2022. Accessed from: https://www.biography.com/actor/katharine-hepburn

Chapter 24

47. Michael Keaton quotes. 2022. Accessed from: https://www.brainyquote.com/authors/michael-keaton-quotes
48. Michael Keaton biography. 2022. Accessed from: https://www.biography.com/actor/michael-keaton

Chapter 25

49. Michelle Pfeiffer quotes. 2022. Accessed from: https://www.brainyquote.com/authors/michelle-pfeiffer-quotes
50. Michelle Pfeiffer biography. 2022. Accessed from: https://www.biography.com/actor/michelle-pfeiffer

Chapter 26

51. James Dean quotes. 2022. Accessed from: https://www.brainyquote.com/authors/james-dean-quotes
52. James Dean biography. 2022. Accessed from: https://www.biography.com/actor/james-dean

Chapter 27

53. Kevin Hart quotes. 2022. Accessed from: https://www.brainyquote.com/authors/kevin-hart-quotes

54. Kevin Hart biography. 2022. Accessed from: https://www.biography.com/performer/kevin-hart

Chapter 28

55. Conan O'Brien quotes. 2022. Accessed from: https://www.brainyquote.com/authors/conan-obrien-quotes
56. Conan O'Brien biography. 2022. Accessed from: https://www.biography.com/performer/conan-obrien

Chapter 29

57. Jon Stewart quotes. 2022. Accessed from: https://www.brainyquote.com/authors/jon-stewart-quotes
58. Jon Stewart biography. 2022. Accessed from: https://www.biography.com/media-figure/jon-stewart

Chapter 30

59. Lucy Ball quotes. 2022. Accessed from: https://www.brainyquote.com/authors/lucille-ball-quotes
60. Lucy Ball biography. 2022. Accessed from: https://www.biography.com/actor/lucille-ball

Chapter 31

61. Charlie Chaplain quotes. 2022. Accessed from: https://www.brainyquote.com/authors/charlie-chaplin-quotes
62. Charlie Chaplain biography. 2022. Accessed from: https://www.biography.com/actor/charlie-chaplin

Chapter 32

63. Danny DeVito quotes. 2022. Accessed from: https://www.brainyquote.com/authors/danny-devito-quotes
64. Danny DeVito biography. 2022. Accessed from: https://www.biography.com/actor/danny-devito

Chapter 33

65. Steven Spielberg quotes. 2022. Accessed from: https://www.brainyquote.com/authors/steven-spielberg-quotes
66. Steven Spielberg biography. 2022. Accessed from: https://www.biography.com/filmmaker/steven-spielberg

Chapter 34

67. George Lucas quotes. 2022. Accessed from: https://www.brainyquote.com/authors/george-lucas-quotes
68. George Lucas biography. 2022. Accessed from: https://www.biography.com/filmmaker/george-lucas

Chapter 35

69. Spike Lee quotes. 2022. Accessed from: https://www.brainyquote.com/authors/spike-lee-quotes
70. Spike Lee biography. 2022. Accessed from: https://www.biography.com/media-figure/spike-lee

Chapter 36

71. James Cameron quotes. 2022. Accessed from: https://www.brainyquote.com/authors/james-cameron-quotes
72. James Cameron biography. 2022. Accessed from: https://www.biography.com/filmmaker/james-cameron

Chapter 37

73. Quentin Tarantino quotes. 2022. Accessed from: https://www.brainyquote.com/authors/quentin-tarantino-quotes
74. Quentin Tarantino biography. 2022. Accessed from: https://www.biography.com/filmmaker/quentin-tarantino

Chapter 38

75. Walt Disney quotes. 2022. Accessed from: https://www.brainyquote.com/authors/walt-disney-quotes
76. Walt Disney biography. 2022. Accessed from: https://www.biography.com/business-figure/walt-disney

Chapter 39

77. Stan Lee quotes. 2022. Accessed from: https://www.brainyquote.com/authors/stan-lee-quotes
78. Stan Lee biography. 2022. Accessed from: https://www.biography.com/media-figure/stan-lee

Chapter 40

79. Oprah Winfrey quotes. 2022. Accessed from: https://www.brainyquote.com/authors/oprah-winfrey-quotes

80. Oprah Winfrey biography. 2022. Accessed from: https://www.biography.com/media-figure/oprah-winfrey

Chapter 41

81. Barbara Walters quotes. 2022. Accessed from: https://www.brainyquote.com/authors/barbara-walters-quotes
82. Barbara Walters biography. 2022. Accessed from: https://www.biography.com/media-figure/barbara-walters

Chapter 42

83. Larry King quotes. 2022. Accessed from: https://www.brainyquote.com/authors/larry-king-quotes
84. Larry King biography. 2022. Accessed from: https://www.biography.com/media-figure/larry-king

Chapter 43

85. Tyra Banks quotes. 2022. Accessed from: https://www.brainyquote.com/authors/tyra-banks-quotes
86. Tyra Banks biography. 2022. Accessed from: https://www.biography.com/personality/tyra-banks

Chapter 44

87. Steve Harvey quotes. 2022. Accessed from: https://www.brainyquote.com/authors/steve-harvey-quotes
88. Steve Harvey biography. 2022. Accessed from: https://www.biography.com/personality/steve-harvey

Chapter 45

89. Joan Rivers quotes. 2022. Accessed from: https://www.brainyquote.com/authors/joan-rivers-quotes
90. Joan Rivers biography. 2022. Accessed from: https://www.biography.com/performer/joan-rivers

Chapter 46

91. Whoopi Goldberg quotes. 2022. Accessed from: https://www.brainyquote.com/authors/whoopi-goldberg-quotes
92. Whoopi Goldberg biography. 2022. Accessed from: https://www.biography.com/actor/whoopi-goldberg

About Dr. Rob

Dr. Rob Carpenter—known simply as Dr. Rob—is a #1 international best-selling author, speaker, professor, and filmmaker who miraculously survived a tragic accident and vowed to not only rebuild his life, but to help others rebuild their lives too.

Dr. Rob's works have been featured in The New York Times, Business Insider, and People Magazine and he has been a visiting or part-time professor and lecturer at various universities like UCLA and Syracuse University in LA; previously served at the 2x Emmy Award Winning USC Media Institute for Social Change as well as on numerous television and movie sets as an actor, writer, director, or producer; and is host of The Great Health Debates (formerly Harvard Health TV). He is the creator of e-courses and writes and speaks extensively on a variety of topics including personal transformation, happiness and mental health, leadership development, and inspirational storytelling and storytelling for leaders and executives, among others. His main interest is storytelling that creates personal and social change.

Dr. Rob is the first in his family to graduate from college and his published works have appeared in the Harvard Journal of Public Health and The Oxford Business Review, among other publications.

His 2021 book 'The 48 Laws of Happiness', which is available at Amazon, Barnes and Noble, Walmart, and Target, has been described as "profoundly empathetic" by New York Media critic Kirkus and his 2022 book, 'Red Carpet Manuscript', became the #1 best selling book on Amazon Kindle in multiple categories. His new book series 'Icons & Legends' will debut featuring the top secrets and life lessons from the world's most influential celebrities, athletes, and musicians.

Dr. Rob has multiple movie, television, and comic book series in development. During Superbowl week in 2023, his podcast, Dear Underdog, will debut with co-host Emmy Award winning writer Kayona Ebony Brown featuring inspirational underdog sports stories.

Books By Dr. Rob

Icons & Legends: Success Strategies of the World's Most Successful Celebrities

Red Carpet Manuscript: How Authors Can Bring Their Books To The Big Screen

The 48 Laws of Happiness: Secrets Revealed For Becoming The Happiest You